All Together Now

ALL TOGE

ALAN DOYLE

THER
NOW

DOUBLEDAY CANADA

Doubleday Canada and colophon are registered trademarks of Penguin Random House Canada Limited

Library and Archives Canada Cataloguing in Publication

Title: All together now / Alan Doyle.

Names: Doyle, Alan, 1969- author.
Identifiers: Canadiana (print) 20200331167 | Canadiana (ebook) 20200331469 |
ISBN 9780385696777 (hardcover) | ISBN 9780385696784 (EPUB)
Subjects: LCSH: Doyle, Alan, 1969- —Anecdotes. | LCSH: Great Big Sea
(Musical group)—Anecdotes. | LCSH: Musicians—Newfoundland
and Labrador—Anecdotes. | LCGFT: Anecdotes.
Classification: LCC ML420.D755 A3 2020 | DDC 782.42164092—dc23

Book design: Kelly Hill
Cover photos: Adam Hefferman

Interior images: (ring stains) Davdeka/Shutterstock.com;
all other images Clipart.com.

Lyrics to "Large-Breasted Woman" © Skinner's Hill Music, Ltd.,
administered by Kobalt Music Group Ltd.

Printed and bound in Canada

Published in Canada by Doubleday Canada,
a division of Penguin Random House Canada Limited

www.penguinrandomhouse.ca

10 9 8 7 6 5 4 3 2

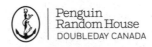

Penguin
Random House
DOUBLEDAY CANADA

This book is dedicated to everyone working
to find a way out of this pandemic and
everyone holding fast on the front lines
to keep us safe while we are still in it.

light tales for heavy times

I AM SUPPOSED to be in Italy.

To be specific, today I am supposed to be in Matera, a wondrous ancient cave city carved into the hills of southern Italy. My bandmates and I were to play a concert here, at the foot of a vineyard on a sandstone bluff dotted with olive trees. I bet the after-show party would have featured rare wines that I could never find or afford even if I could. I'm sure we'd all be beaming as we wandered the winding stone roads at midnight or later, as bands on tour often do, headed for the one garden bar still open. Cold Peroni flowing hand over fist for the Friday faces not yet ready to part with the warm glow of night.

I am not in Italy.

I am not where I am supposed to be or doing what I am supposed to be doing. Just about the entire performing world, from bands to dancers to DJs to circus clowns, would all say the same thing. Like so many in the gig and gathering industry, I am home in my basement, occupying myself as best I can while waiting for the COVID-19 pandemic to pass and the green light to signal that our tour buses can roll once again.

As I type this, it is a Friday in July of 2020. It is my seventeenth Friday in a row without some kind of gig. I suspect this is my lengthiest consecutive streak at home since 1994 and offstage since 1982. Now, I wouldn't want you to think it is all bad. I am enjoying the long-overdue extended family time and sleeping in my own bed. But times like this, suppertime on Friday, when I should be sound checking and watching people form up and down the street around the venue, excited people craning their necks to see who's on the bus, or cloistering at close-by patios with glasses raised and troubles soon to be forgotten for a few hours, I miss it.

I am built for the road. Bandmates have commented that my Petty Harbour Hobbit DNA is genetically programmed to live out of a six-foot-long by thirty-inch-wide tour bus bunk and sleep soundly while a diesel engine pushes a forty-five-foot tube on rubber tires through the Canadian winter. Being in one place for this long is not what I am accustomed to, at all. I miss the gigs and the crowds and the physical and mental satisfaction that comes with singing a song while others sing along with you. I miss looking across the stage to wink at a bandmate who's just played something incredible, or giggling as one of them, or more likely I, play or sing a note so wrong that it almost derails the whole train.

I miss the concerts and all that comes with such a privileged life, but I also miss the gatherings. Not just on the road, but at home as well. I live in St. John's, Newfoundland, a city with one of the few great pub cultures in North America. We Newfoundlanders are *sociaholics,* if you'll forgive a generalization. Gathering is our superpower. We do it at home or abroad. We do it in good times and especially in bad. We find each other and congregate and talk and joke and complain and sing. I think this could be why COVID-19 hurts us so badly. It has taken away the one sure-fire defence we have used against so many hardships of history: We get together. We work it out. We get through it. We do what has to be done. Then, we celebrate. With the best of them.

COVID-19 has born us our kryptonite. We can't get together. Not to talk or joke. Not to complain or sing. Not to work it out and get through it. And certainly not to celebrate. For a gathering pub culture like ours, this has been especially hard.

If you are at all like me, you are longing for a pub, with a black and golden pint on the bar and another one not too far behind. Where friends play a game of "Sure, that's nothing" as we try to constantly one-up the story that's just been offered to the gang. Where all the mouths at the table are moving at the same time and no one seems to mind. Where one yarn leads to another so quickly you have to be as ready as an Olympian at the start line to get your tale in before someone else is well into theirs.

Alas, right now, all we can do is imagine such a time.

So why don't we do just that, Dear Reader? Why don't we imagine we are in such a pub—all together, now—and the stories are flying? Let's say we are mid-stride on a Friday, jammed into the corner at the Duke of Duckworth on the last bar stool, my left arm on the bar and my right on the high table. The whole pub before me. The best piece of real estate on Earth tonight.

The musings to follow are offered just as they would be from that throne of a stool. Told in response to a prompt or question or nudge or dare. Told as they occur to me, sometimes to make a point, and more often for no rhyme or reason other than they might make someone laugh and help turn a good night into a great one.

Perhaps a few stories will not only pass the time but get us a little closer to a time when we can do this for real.

I will be there with bells on. Till then, thanks for joining me here.

Cheers,
Alan

It always seems like an innocent enough idea to assemble the gang right after work. "Just pop in for one on the way home. You know, before you gets back to your own house and gets too settled in. You'll be home by five thirty at the latest."

Jerry's still got his suit on. Pulling at his tie like a kidnapped fella in a chair trying to undo the ropes behind his back. He is excited about his first trip to New York, as he's headed there on a work trip in a few weeks. I'm happy to tell him about some of my times there.

As I lift my voice over the din of the Duke, Jerry is holding a pint like it is the Holy Grail and the liquid inside it the antidote to a global pandemic.

Perhaps he is right on both counts.

THE BLIND MAN
✦ & the Can ✦

GREAT BIG SEA landed an amazing gig to perform on Canada Day 2000, right in the middle of Central Park in New York City.

I have always been fascinated with Manhattan, and Central Park in particular. As a kid I would seek out maps of Manhattan and wonder at the rows and rows of perfectly straight numbered streets and avenues. There was not a single piece of straight road anywhere in my young life in Petty Harbour, and barely any along the ex-cow paths turned roadways of St. John's. A perfect urban grid seemed absurd—especially one lined with skyscrapers. Tallest building I'd seen before my twenties was the eleven-storey Confederation Building in St. John's, and there was only one. But in the middle of Manhattan, there were hundreds of them, and many times taller. How did the sun get in? How did you see the edge of town with all the tall buildings around? How did you know where you were without a beach, an ocean, a river or a hill to serve as a guide? Though I had seen parts of the city in hundreds of movies and TV shows, I had trouble imagining what Manhattan actually looked like in person.

And there on the map, right in the middle of this impossible Gotham of straight lines of streets and towers reaching into the clouds, was this green rectangle. I remember noticing it on a map in a schoolbook in Grade 6 or 7 and thinking it must be a mistake or the handiwork of a mischievous classmate who'd coloured over a chunk of Manhattan with a green marker. I looked closer. It was real. I counted the numbered streets that bordered it and quickly realized how enormous the green rectangle must actually be. How could a city so big, so brimming with concrete and brick and pavement, save so much space for one park? I found the very thought of it baffling. I would have to see it for myself, I supposed.

On GBS's first visit to NYC a few years earlier, we played in Lower Manhattan at the famous Bottom Line. It was a quick in and out and I did not get a chance to go to the park. So here on July 1, 2000, not long after my thirtieth birthday, the same me that drew his finger over the green rectangle in the schoolbook was not only going to see Central Park for real, he was going to play a gig there. I was beyond excited.

As well as a wanderlust dream come true, that day in the park was an incredible opportunity for our band's introduction in the United States. Thousands of expat Canadians would throng to the iconic park to celebrate the True North Strong and Free in the heart of the US. If we were ever to tour successfully and make a cent in America, we'd need every single one of these Canucks on our side. And today was a day to impress them.

We'd also get a chance to impress and hopefully befriend the two other bands on the bill, as an association with either of them would boost our visibility. We were opening for The Tragically Hip, perhaps the biggest and most internationally successful Canadian rock band on the road at the time. The Hip had sold millions and millions of records, had dozens of music videos in heavy rotation and had even played on *Saturday Night Live*. When we arrived, many of the Hip crew guys were unloading what seemed like an insane amount of equipment, filling up the backstage area with dozens of road cases and cables. We were still a four-folk-instrument, four-guy band. All our gear and luggage could fit in a medium-sized car.

The band strolled in for their sound check and we got to say quick hellos and chat with guitarists Robbie and Paul, bass player Gord and drummer Johnny. They were very kind and polite gents who did their best not to be annoyed with how excited we were to have this gig, one of the biggest in our career so far, but one of the many gigs they were doing at this level all the time.

When lead singer Gord Downie showed up, I became aware for the first time that he was an impossibly tall person. This towering, honest-to-God Rock Star, accompanied by a large, honest-to-God muscly security person, made for a most impressive and intimidating presence. I wasn't sure we were allowed to talk to him, so I hovered on the sidelines as he chatted with the other guys in the band. Then Robbie turned and pointed me out to Gord.

Gord got taller as he approached, and the muscly security fella got musclier. I stood as tall as I could, but I was dwarfed by them both. Then Gord extended his hand from his long, long arm.

"Hello. I'm Gord. You are the guys from Newfoundland, I hear. Very nice to meet you and have you on the gig."

I was shaking Gord Downie's hand. Backstage. In Central Park. New York City. Holy Shite!

"Hey, yeah, I'm Alan. Big fan of yours for a long time. So glad to be here."

"Have a good show." He turned to go.

"Yeah, it's a big one," I added.

Gord slowed his exit just long enough to poetically add, "It's a walk in the park." And then he turned with the muscly fella and disappeared.

In my mind, this first encounter with The Hip was quite successful: did not geek out too much; just the right amount of giddy to be there. Well done.

This is in the bag, I figured. We totally got this.

Oh dear.

Also on the bill was perhaps the most recognizable Canadian musician in the world at the time: Jeff Healey. Jeff was still riding a wave of popularity from his appearance in the Patrick Swayze film *Road House*. He played the blind leader of the house band, a role that would come to him naturally as he had unfortunately lost his sight to a rare form of eye cancer as a very young boy. He was internationally revered as one of the blues guitar greats of the day.

We didn't get to meet him before his set, which was after ours and before The Hip's. But after slaying the place with his massive hit "See the Light," he was led backstage by a gent I assumed helped Jeff with his touring and travelling as a visually impaired person. As they neared us, I heard Jeff say that he was cool, and the gent went back to the stage to grab some of Jeff's gear.

I guess Jeff could hear us close to him as he turned our way.

Trying to get ahead of any awkwardness, I jumped in.

"Hey, Jeff. It's Alan and Darrell from Great Big Sea here." I was not sure if I should put my hand out or not. Would he know it was out there? Would that be weird? I wasn't sure.

"Loved your set, man," Darrell said, saving the moment as he extended his hand just as Jeff extended his.

"Thanks, fellas. You guys just played, right? With the accordions and stuff? Love that stuff, man," says Guitar God.

"Really? Thanks, man. So cool of you to say." I was chuffed.

"Yeah, I love it when music is attached to a place, like the blues is to certain parts of the South. And nothing in Canada sounds like what you guys got going on out there on the Rock. Great stuff, man."

This was going even better than the meeting with The Hip guys.

Home run.

Oh dear.

"Hey, Jeff. Can I get you something? A beer or whatever." Darrell was on fire!

Jeff looked a little bashful and replied, "Man, I really gotta take a piss. You know where the can is?"

Me and Darrell looked at each other with matching, unspoken, yet unmistakable looks that screamed, I HAVE NEVER TAKEN A BLIND PERSON, MUCH LESS A WICKED FAMOUS BLIND PERSON, TO THE BATHROOM. HOW DO YOU DO IT? WHAT HAPPENS IN THERE? I AM HAPPY TO DO WHATEVER IS REQUIRED BUT WHAT EXACT DUTIES AM I AGREEING TO? Then, almost instantly, we both said,

"Yes, b'y."

Darrell, being closest to Jeff, offered his arm as the Guitar God offered his hand. Darrell led him through the maze of road cases and coils of audio and lighting cables snaking throughout the backstage area. I watched as my friend, a daydreamer like myself, who wasted as much time as me in class fantasizing about meeting and becoming a famous musician, now led one of the most famous guitarists in the world to the can. It was a true sign that we had made it. Part of the way, at least.

Darrell turned the knob on the single bathroom door and held it open as Jeff stepped in. I watched as Darrell hesitated and shot me a look that said, WHAT THE F—K DO I DO NOW?

I shrugged.

Darrell took half a step into the small bathroom with Jeff just as the door was closing. It bumped Darrell's leg and held the door ajar. A most surprised and awkward look came over Jeff's face.

"Ah. That's cool, man. I can handle it from here."

"Oh yeah, of course. For sure. Deadly. I'll just wait here for you, I s'pose." Darrell took a step back, almost tripping over a cable.

"Great." Guitar God looked a little unsure.

Darrell closed the door for him and stood by for just a second, the noble sentinel, until he noticed that the bathroom light switch, fixed next to him on the outside of the stall, was in the off position.

He flicked it on.

I started waving and jumping from across the cases, yell-whispering, "Darrell! Hey!"

He noticed me right away. "What?!"

I waved him towards me with one hand—that nervous, angry kind of wave with way too many flapping motions towards yourself—while I pressed the first finger of my other hand to my lips, yell-whispering, "SHH!"

I was too upset and anxious to form a full sentence. "The light?! Jesus Christ, b'y."

Darrell made a face like maybe it was no big deal and I was maybe overreacting. "I'm sure it's fine. Honest mistake. Relax, b'y."

But I could not relax. "You knows he can hear you flicking it on, with that heightened other sense thing blind fellas got. And, Holy Frig, there's probably a ceiling fan connected to the light! Jesus, he's in there thinking we're out here having a grand laugh at him now."

I was not sticking around to make my point to Darrell any further, or to listen to him make his. Quickly and determinedly, I tiptoed to the bathroom to undo his foolish mistake.

When I reached the bathroom door, I pressed my ear and heard either pee or water-running sounds. All seemed well enough in there.

So I switched the light back off.

Right away I heard Darrell yell-whispering my name. I spun around to see him, his mouth wide open, hand on his forehead, waving the other in a fit of frustrated puzzlement. "What in the Jaysus is the good of that?"

"Right. Holy shite. Stupid." I smacked myself in the head. What a moronic thing to do. I had just made the whole situation worse. I panicked. I had to do something to fix this mess I'd made.

So I switched the light back on.

Darrell was dancing with angry disbelief when I heard the squeak of the bathroom door open behind me. His colour went white as a sheet as he saw the look on Jeff's face.

"Couple of jokers, hey."

"Oh hey, man," I said, hoping to brush over the whole deal. "Can I help you back across the stage and get you a beer and we can pick right up where we left off on that chat 'cause that was really cool and what you were saying about the blues and that was amazing."

"I think I'm good, fellas."

And the Guitar God turned and walked through the black curtain separating the side stage from the loading area.

I hung my head and walked back through the snakes of cables and piles of cases to where Darrell was standing, shoulders slumped, shaking his head to the sky. He smacked me as hard as he could upside my head. I swear I almost asked for a second one.

Oh dear, indeed.

I never met or spoke to Jeff Healey again and, like most in the Canadian music community, was saddened to learn of his far-too-soon passing in 2008. I have heard only great things about this gentle and kind man. I have never heard of him saying a bad word about anyone. But I would not be one bit surprised to learn that somewhere, sometime, someone mentioned Alan Doyle or GBS to Jeff Healey. And Jeff Healey would have been totally justified if he replied something like this:

"Great Big Sea fellas? What a bunch of dicks."

*My friend Mary's got exactly ninety minutes
before she has to be home to relieve her babysitter.
She shines in her slim ready-for-court lawyer black
skirt and blazer over a smart grey vest and white
blouse that has somehow retained its crisp, sharp
corners since she ironed it almost half a day ago.
She's a super mom. One of the most impressive
stereotypes, I think. From rural Newfoundland but
settled in St. John's after she graduated from
Memorial University of Newfoundland and then
Dalhousie Law. She has to get her two beer in
before bolting for home to "feed three generations.
My aunt is in town having a procedure done at the
hospital, so the house is in slings."*

She pauses to drain the last of her Corona.

*"That's what I gets for being the only relative
in town, I suppose."*

*My brother, Bernie, and I look at each
other across a table of pint glasses and say,*

"Uncle Reg."

UNCLE REG

UNCLE REG WAS one of the regular visitors to our house in Petty Harbour, as he had a myriad of health problems that required frequent visits to the St. John's area for attention.

My mom's oldest brother was a wonderful tall, lanky fella of well over six feet, much like his younger brother, my uncle Bob. The Doyles of Petty Harbour are not particularly a tall breed, so my uncles from Marystown always looked like Goliaths to me. Reg, in particular, looked like a giant sorcerer who'd just taken off his pointy hat, revealing a balding head with just a few hairs on one side combed over to the other. His long arms, which had not an ounce of fat along the sinews of muscle that ran from his short shirt-sleeves to his wrists, looked perfect for casting spells, especially when they waved and spun about when he drank too much. Which was quite often. I kept expecting lightning to shoot from his index finger when he'd point it to the sky after slamming a card to the kitchen table during a game of 120s hard enough to wake the dead.

"Take that, ye bastards!" he would shout, sending his false teeth sliding out his mouth before he licked them back into place with his long, lizard-like tongue.

His supernatural status was bolstered by the fact that we believed all his legendary hunting and fishing tales. Little did we kids know our parents were rolling their eyes behind us while he held us spellbound.

"I caught eight trout yesterday in about ten minutes. All on the one worm. And when I finished, I put that worm back under the rock where I found him. I swear to Jesus he winked at me before he bore back down in the ground," Reg said, pointing to the ground with a lanky finger and winking with a wrinkled eye. "And the size of the trout! All's I can tell ye is that I couldn't lug 'em all the one time. I brought them up to the truck two by two. That's all I could manage. And when I finally got the seventh and eighth one up to the truck, I couldn't fit the bastards in the back. Had to sit two of them up in the cab next to me with the seat belt wrapped around them. I'd say I'll be eating them till next spring."

Me and Bernie looked at each other, silently nodding in agreement that this was not only likely but wicked cool.

No wonder we thought him capable of superhuman activity. A stubborn moose once took two of his bullets in the neck but refused to lie down. "I chased that bastard till me boots were full of sweat, yelling at him the whole time, 'You're not getting away with my hard-earned bullets!' I ran him down to the edge of the pond and he finally stopped. Turned round his head and I was sure he would drop there on the beach. Well no, b'y, he gets this defiant look in his eye that just says, 'No b'y. Not today.' And with that he jumps in the pond and starts kicking and paddling across for all he's worth.

"Well all I could see was me two bullets gone to waste and I couldn't have that, so I ran up to the highest rock I could find, and I dove, sweaty boots and all, as high and as far as I could."

Uncle Reg bent forward now and assumed a Superman flying position.

"Well I landed right on the bastard's back and rode him right around in a circle like a cowboy on a wild buck. He headed back from where we came and was still twisting and lifting when we got to the beach. I figured he would give up for sure, but the bastard starts galloping as fast as he can. Jesus, we must have gone a quarter-mile when he finally starts to give in. I'm holding on to his antlers and what do I see in the distance but the truck! I steered his head in that direction, and I'll be f—ked if he didn't turn and start walking that way. I steered him left and right as the path bent back and forth to the truck.

"I was like Willie God-Damned Shoemaker up there.

"When we got to the back of truck, I slid off his back. I didn't want to be shooting off the gun that close to the road, so I was glad when the poor bastard dropped to the ground right there and then. Pretty agreeable, he was. I'm sure if he had one more breath, he would have opened the tailgate for me. And if he had two, he would have jumped in."

Me and Bernie looked at each other, silently nodding in agreement that this was not only possible but happened pretty much as described. Reg was strong as a bull and tough as a boot. Any one of the many injuries and illnesses he encountered would have killed a mortal, we figured.

My father once said of Reg's strength and resilience, "You could run Reg over with a cement mixer and when you stopped to check on him, he'd already be up off the pavement, down on one knee to make sure he hadn't knocked the base off the bottom of 'er with his head."

We all figured nothing could ever befall him. Fate's many attempts to bring him down were all thwarted by his heroic hardiness: Pneumonia cast aside by a hot toddy. Congestion shook off by a hard cough and a couple of fists to the chest. As Fate could not beat him, it did the only thing it could. It started removing him. Bit by bit.

———

Fate took its first few cuts of Uncle Reg on top of a hill in Marystown, Newfoundland, in a makeshift sawmill he erected out back of his house. Although "makeshift" does not accurately describe the contraption he assembled.

Reg's house was nothing short of spectacular. He was an incredible woodworker and could make anything from a rough workbench to an armoire fit for royalty, and his beautifully crafted doors, cupboards, tables and desks decorated the home he'd built for himself and his family. A walk through the halls of that house was like a trip to the Governor General's residence as far as we Petty Harbour kids were concerned.

In stark contrast, the barn-like structure in the back that housed his sawmill was bare and simple, not unlike something you might see on any farm. There was one massive difference, though: Uncle Reg's barn had a hole in one wall the exact size of a 1977 Dodge pickup. I know this because right there, jutting out from a wall, was a 1977 Dodge pickup. It was as though someone had careened off the road, spun a circle or two and then drove the tailgate of the truck right through the side of the barn. Even more odd was the fact that the tail and flatbed had been torn off, leaving the long driveshaft exposed. On further inspection, you could see fitted to the tip of the driveshaft a thick steel disc with large, razor-sharp teeth.

"That's the biggest saw blade I ever saw!" I was afraid to touch it but could not take my eyes off it.

"Yes, my son," Reg said, rubbing his hands. "That could cut a twenty-four-inch log down in seconds. Just let me jump in the truck and start her up."

He proudly slipped through a crack in the wall and hopped into the rusty cab of the truck. He turned a key, and the engine started, first flick.

"Mind your hands now!" he shouted, pressing his foot to

the accelerator. The blade spun with dangerous speed. He reached to the floor and grabbed a rock about the size of an American football and lay it on the gas pedal, then slipped back into the barn, leaving the engine running and blade spinning full blast. I swear you could have cut a German tank in half in ten seconds.

"Like a James Bond movie!" Bernie shouted at me over the din.

"What?!" I leaned in.

"Like a James Bond movie! Where they try to kill the spy buddy!"

Reg could hear us, no problem. "Yes, Jesus, you'd split James Bond and Scarface and the friggin' Grinch right down the middle right there I'd say!"

I was transfixed by the blade as they continued to yell-chat.

Bernie, ever the engineer even as a kid, said, "So it's a direct-drive thing?! Full pedal, full spin?!"

Reg, leaning way too close to the blade, "Yes, drop a rock on the pedal and let her go full on till she runs out of gas!"

"And is there any gears?!"

"Yes, my son! One gear. High gear!"

"And do you have a safety switch or emergency-off pedal or something!? You know, if something goes wrong?!"

The lack of response made me look to Reg. He had an expression on his face that so clearly told me he'd just been asked a question that had never once occurred to him.

Mom hung up the phone after receiving the news and shouted what would be a recurring, all-too familiar call. "Reg's on the way in to Emergency. I dare say he'll be in here for the night. So pull out the couch."

Fate had taken two of Reg's fingers in the mill after his shirtsleeve got hooked in the nub of a bow and pulled his hand into the blade, severing the middle two fingers on his left hand.

Later that night, after his trip to Emergency, Reg strolled in our back-porch door with a bandage on one hand and a bottle of rum in the other. The doctors had managed to reattach part of one finger, but it left him with the most peculiar drinking hand, as he called it. In a day or so he'd have the bandages off and be back at the 120s table, slamming down a trump with his good hand while the other, recently mangled one wrapped what fingers it had left around a rum glass.

I can still picture him clutching the glass of black rum and Coke with his newly chiselled claw. His thumb was fine, pressed against one side of the glass to steady his drink. But on the other side, where four long, straight fingers should be, was a grotesque mash of swollen fingers and half-fingers and fingers that were missing altogether: Near the rim of the glass, a swollen index finger wrapped around the circumference of the glass and almost touched the tip of the thumb. On the base of the glass was a badly broken pinky with a number of stitches oozing what I hoped was blood. But it was between these two fingers that the real horror show played out.

His middle finger was, well, not there. Its stub stuck to the glass with a bloody tip, leaving nothing but a ghoulish space between the index and the ring finger. And as for his ring finger, two-thirds stuck straight out and was clearly missing its tip. It looked like they had sewn it back on, if "they" were a couple of drunken fellas on the back of a speeding moving van. Rough black stitches were crudely tied off and flesh was forced back together like the edge of a catcher's mitt. "Frankenstein finger," I whispered to no one.

"I'm not sure what's grosser," my sister Kim said with a face like someone had just let one go, "the fingers that're there or the ones that aren't."

Reg would get a few more fingers nipped and arms and legs gashed in that sawmill, but Fate was not satisfied with the pace of his bit-by-bit disappearance.

So Fate took a chainsaw to his face.

Yes, that's correct. Fate would have it that while deep in the woods, Reg's chainsaw bucked just as he slipped on a wet bow. The spinning chain blades passed through his cheek into his mouth, cutting off half his tongue and almost passing through the other side of his face.

"Reg's on the way in to Emergency. I dare say he'll be in here for the night. So pull out the couch."

A day or so later Reg strolled in the back door with a bottle of rum in one mangled hand and "a face on him like Freddy Krueger," we all agreed. Including Reg.

So now Reg was down a finger and a half, half a tongue, a few teeth and about a third of a side of his face.

But Fate was not finished with him yet. I imagine Fate felt there was still too much of him in one spot.

So Fate gave him stomach cancer.

Yes, that's correct. Fate gave him the kind of cancer that was treated by, you guessed it, removal of part of his stomach and "other bits of guts, I suppose," as Reg described it. The procedure was to happen immediately.

Not long later came a familiar call from the kitchen.

"Reg's on the way in to Emergency. I dare say he'll be in here for the night. So pull out the couch."

A week or so later Reg strolled in the back door with a bottle of rum in his mangled hand, a grin on his chopped-up face and a zipper in his chest from chin to bellybutton.

We all figured he was not long for this world, but he seemed unfazed by the whole deal. No facts of the matter could break his stride. Hard as nails.

To keep the chat light, me and my brother spoke one after the other as he sipped his rum.

"Jesus, Uncle Reg. You're half the man you used to be."

"Yes, b'y, they're getting rid of you one part at a time."

"There are more parts of you somewhere else."

He rubbed his two-fingered hand over his half-face and

said with the certainty of someone who knew something no one else did,

"Or I suppose I could be just rebuilding meself somewhere else."

Me and Bernie looked at each other silently. And then we nodded in agreement that we found this not only possible but quite likely.

Over Perry's shoulder I can see the one thing about the Duke I often wish was not there: the TVs. I don't watch much TV, so when I see one I tend to stare at it longer than I want. A friggin' sports channel has made me miss the first part of Perry's story, which already has everyone rolling. I pick it up mid-stride.

"And then we got tickets to the game." Perry points to me and I realize that he was taken by an ad on the TV for the Grey Cup game, and he's launched into a tale of one of the greatest weekends of our lives.

I watch him act it out as he poses athletically in a quarterback stance before quickly transitioning to his half-of-a-waltz dance: one low hand wrapped around an imaginary partner's waist, and the other held high, his palm forward to lead the way.

I can't resist joining the pantomime, and jump from the throne, extend my hand and bow.

"Could I have this dance?"

Anne Murray & THE GREY CUP

OVER THE YEARS, I've experienced some ridiculously Canadian moments. Having a flight cancelled in St. John's because moose had climbed the airport snowdrifts and were licking salt off the runway. Watching my pee run up Magnetic Hill near Moncton. Hearing Sidney Crosby's winning shout before the crowd erupted at the gold medal hockey game at the Vancouver Olympics, and weeping at the Duke of Duckworth pub as the Newfoundland and Labrador rink won the Olympic gold in curling. But as Canuck as all these experiences sound, I have one story that may be the best one-two punch experience in Canadian history.

On Sunday, November 25, 2007, the Grey Cup final was played in Toronto at what many still call the SkyDome.

There was a huge celebration over the weekend that included appearances by Lenny Kravitz, Barenaked Ladies, Trailer Park Boys and Great Big Sea, and I had convinced a couple of my oldest pals—Perry and Greg—to join us. Perry and I had met in Petty Harbour when we were four and have been pals ever since. These days, he writes and works on TV shows like *Republic of Doyle*, *Frontier* and *Caught*. I met Greg when I was about eleven and he was the other goalie in the local minor hockey program and we quickly discovered we were both musicians. Greg played drums in my first band, First Attempt, and he's currently the principal percussionist in the smash-hit musical *Come From Away*. Over the years we have gotten up to some fun shenanigans and I was glad to have them along.

We sat in a fancy box overlooking the field with Brent Butt and Mike and the Trailer Park Boys gang, watching Lenny Kravitz slay the place. I am not completely proud of the brazen attitude that came over me in those final seconds of the game, but all this famous company, and maybe a few bevvies, made me feel emboldened, and I wanted to make a great night out for the lads. When the final buzzer went and the Saskatchewan Roughriders won the game, I said to my pals matter-of-factly, "Let's go down on the field."

Perry and I had been through a lot. We cut out cod tongues together at age ten. We scampered down dangerous cliffs to look at skin mags at twelve. We graduated high school together and lived together during university. I stood next to him when he got married, and he stood next to me when I did the same.

"Yeah, let's go hoist the Cup," Perry said, assuming I was joking.

"You're not serious? Is he serious?" Greg said. He was always a bit of a worrier.

Perry looked over and studied me for a moment. He must have seen a familiar look in my eye. "Yes. Yes, he is."

As the on-field post-game celebration started, I made for the staff elevator. I had the button pushed before Greg could protest.

"Keep your passes held up."

About laminated passes on lanyards: if wielded properly, they can be powerful. I know this from experience—I cannot tell you how many times I've walked into the back of one of our gigs with a dodgy pass from the last night's venue as a security guard looked at his phone. You won't fool the White House staff, but a confident walk and a flash of some plastic thing hanging around your neck will get you backstage at four-fifths of the festivals on Earth.

The Grey Cup passes that Perry, Greg and I were wearing read "ENTERTAINMENT," or something like that. Along the bottom were our assigned seats and limitations. "Cover the bottom with your finger when you holds it up," I whispered, pulling Greg onto the staff elevator.

Just as the door was about to close, a fella wearing a full black suit and an earpiece got on the elevator and held the door for a gent who must have been a Cabinet minister or something. The fella in the black suit looked to us dubiously, but I held up the ENTERTAINMENT pass. He nodded and asked, "Field level as well?"

"Yes, sir."

I wasn't lying, I figured. He hadn't ask if we were *allowed* on the field level. Or if we had any business at all on the field level. Or if the passes we had just flashed were for a Canadian Tire fundraising event from three years previous.

The elevator stopped three times on the way down, each time filling up with reporters, and what seemed to be family of team members. I thought we'd be caught for sure.

When we finally reached the field level, we were greeted by a security fella named Hal. "Reporters to the corral on the right, please, and families follow the green line to the Green Room and someone will come get you from there."

"Herded like cattle,'" one of the reporters said. He eyed my pass suspiciously as he left with the herd.

"Headed to the VIP exit?" Hal asked the man with the earpiece. "They coming down with you?" he said, pointing to us.

Secret Service fella was listening to something in his ear and nodded. Hal stepped out of the way, and I strode from that elevator like someone who'd just been introduced as a winner at the Grammys.

"We're gonna get shot," Greg whisper-yelled.

"Just keep walking."

As we walked through the tunnel to the field, I did my best to make eye contact with every security person along the way, smiling a smile that I hoped said, "Yeah, Hal just let us in. You want to go talk to Hal and piss him off, you are welcome to, but I wouldn't mess with Hal." It must have worked because next thing I knew we were rounding the corner under the bleachers and the lights of the field came into full view.

About twenty strides from the green Astroturf, I saw the Roughrider players making their way towards us, in full celebration.

"Hey, why do they get to go on?!" I turned to hear a voice in a crowd trapped behind a rope. Cameras and microphones in hand, this was clearly the reporters' area, and there at the edge of the rope was the cranky little fella from the elevator. He was onto us.

"Don't break stride, fellas," I said. A security guard walked our way, but I held up the pass and pointed to a pile of audio equipment on the edge of the field. I'm pretty sure it was Lenny Kravitz's gear. The security guard nodded and went back to more pressing matters.

"Hey, Great Big Sea!" I turned to see one of the players rushing my way.

"Yeah, man, congrats! Way to go!" I said.

"Woo! Kiss it!" he shouted.

"Excuse me?" I was happy for him but not that happy. What did he mean anyway?

"Kiss it!" He lay the Grey Cup trophy in my arms. "Yeah! Kiss it!"

I don't know what you do when a sweaty 325-pound man hands you a silver cup and says, "Kiss it." But I can tell you that I embraced and kissed that Cup like it was my fiancée.

And as quickly as that, he and the Cup were gone and we were awash in green jerseys as the team joyously barrelled past us to the dressing room. I turned to find Greg and Perry, grinning ear to ear. It was a proud moment. Except that right there, about a hundred feet behind Greg and Perry, I saw him approaching from the tunnel. Quickly. He held a walkie-talkie to his mouth.

It was Hal.

I grabbed the lads and we crossed the field to the first exit sign I could see. As we reached it, a kind fella in a yellow security vest asked if he could help us.

"Yes, sir. We are looking for the, ah, ah . . ." I stuttered, but Perry and Greg remembered the right thing to say.

"The VIP exit." They held their passes high, covering the bottom half like we had practised, and the guard pointed to the exit, not five strides away.

My heart filled with pride.

———

Having kissed the grail and dodged a bullet, we made our way into the late night of the Big Smoke. What followed that evening was your typical happenings of a lads' night on the lash. From the Grey Cup game we went to a late ceremony at a nearby Holy House to confess our sins to the high powers on the altar. One member of our group was so racked with guilt he was almost drawn into a private confessional, since a general absolution would not provide him with the necessary relief. Feeling much better, we left the Holy House and went to a local library to read up on the classics and current events, followed by a relaxing session of yoga. We then drifted off into a peaceful sleep at around 11 p.m.

Or something like that.

I woke on Monday morning with a feeling of slight nausea, headache and dry mouth. Must have been the hot dogs at the game, I supposed. I made my way to the hotel lobby in search of medicinal caffeine and noticed some of the Trailer Park Boys waiting near the concierge. After some morning pleasantries, I learned that they were suffering from many of the same symptoms as I. That confirmed it. It must have been the hot dogs at the game.

They explained they were heading back East. I should have said something like, "Oh too bad. We're sticking around for a few more nights. You guys could really keep the party going." However, my malaise afforded me no Maritimes pleasantries, and I thought, "Thank f—k." I know the TPB boys understand.

There would be no quiet night for me, as GBS agreed to sing a few songs for the Gilda's Club charity concert. Greg had a symphony gig or something, but Perry stuck around as the band and I would be performing with an all-star roster of Canadian talent, among them the legendary Anne Murray. I'd briefly crossed paths with her at an East Coast Music Awards a number of years ago but had never seen her perform in person, and I was certain she'd never seen me. I was excited to meet her since she was worshipped in my house and probably every other house in Atlantic Canada. She was a bona fide International Rock Star. She still is.

We had a quick sound check at the Elgin Theatre at around 2 p.m. No big deal as we were just going to sing a couple of a cappella tunes that night. After the sound check, the other band members returned to the hotel, but I stuck around, hoping to catch a glimpse of the Legend.

It was all low-key and casual in the theatre, until the stage lady approached me and asked if I knew any Anne Murray tunes. I told her, 'Madam, I'm from Petty Harbour, Newfoundland, so I knows every Anne Murray tune." She then asked if I'd mind joining Anne singing "Could I Have This Dance" for the finale.

Would I *mind* singing "Could I Have This Dance" with Anne Murray?

"No, love. I don't think I'd mind that at all," I said.

Holy shite—l am going to sing live onstage with Anne Friggin' Murray, I said to myself.

The band reassembled at the theatre around six thirty and we sat backstage waiting for the show to start. We sang a couple of tunes when it was our turn to perform, and seemed well received. But not long after, it was time for Anne's performance. I nipped out to the wings to watch Anne's set. Her voice was still perfect. I waited for my cue.

Anne was joined by the most awesome Nelly Furtado to sing "Daydream Believer," and when the song ended, it was time for the finale. Anne began singing, "I'll always remember . . ." and as the chorus came around, I did not hesitate for a second. I walked right to centre stage and joined Nelly and Anne.

I can't recall much about singing with her. All I could think was, "Holy Sweet Jesus, somebody take my picture onstage with Anne Friggin' Murray." One of my sisters is a medical professional, the other is getting her third degree in post-secondary education, and my brother is an engineer with an MBA to boot. This was my one and only chance to get to the top of the gravy bowl order in our house.

As the chorus repeated, Anne stepped back and gave me a knowing nod and a gentle pat on the back. I humbly responded, nodding back in that "nicely sung, we're in this song together" kind of way, and oh so respectfully patted her on the back, giving her a quick but certain Newfoundland wink. A moment later, applause roared through the hall.

And Anne Murray was gone.

After the concert, Perry and I walked back to the hotel. The same two kids who'd beat the paths of Petty Harbour now strolling down the down the biggest street in the world. As the previous night had been large, we were now headed for a Tim Hortons sandwich and bed.

"A Tim Hortons sandwich after a gig in Toronto," I said to my childhood friend as we turned off Yonge Street and walked towards the King Edward Hotel. "What's more Canadian than that?"

"What's more Canadian than that?" Perry stopped and pointed his finger at me and then to the heavens for effect.

"You laid your hands on the Grey Cup and Anne Murray in less than twenty-four hours."

Oh Canada.

The bar at the Duke is altar enough for me. This gathering of people sharing love and joy is all the Mass I need. It is early yet, but the hymns will come later and Scott behind the bar will hear any confession you wish to offer.

As I wait for my pint to settle, he commends me on my patience. "That's the proper way for Guinness. Wait a minute and it is way better. You got to stand over it and say a prayer."

Scott is impressed as I recite a Catholic psalm etched into my brain from hundreds and hundreds of Masses in Petty Harbour. He is surprised to hear I hold a university degree in religious studies.

"Who's your favourite fella in the Bible?"

He means it as a joke, I'm sure, and doesn't expect me to respond. But the glow of the bar lights announce that Happy Hour is leading to Happy Hour and a Half. And the confessional is no place to leave a question unanswered.

The FELLA with the VINEGAR SPONGE

"IF YOU COULD have dinner with anyone in history, alive or dead, who would it be?"

If you play in a band for a living or have achieved any level of celebrity, you've likely been asked this question time and again during interviews. Sometimes this question comes during a long-form interview with the expectation of a thoughtful explanation, but more often than not it comes at the end of quick morning FM radio interview in a "speed round" session, where you answer as many questions as you can in a minute. This question might well be preceded by "poutine or pizza?" and followed by "boxers or briefs?"

I almost always offer the same answer, whatever the format. And if my answer perplexes the long-form interviewers, it downright derails the morning FM jocks.

Apologies.

A typical speed-round session involves a hyper-stimulated DJ Buddy who's been up since 4 a.m. and completely blasted on caffeine by our 8:45 a.m. chat. "All right, Alan, got time for a quickie session before you go? Now don't think too hard about the answers—they are meant to be right off the top of your head, so no pausing or stopping. Ready? All right, sixty seconds on the clock and let's go!"

The questions come rapid-fire and are meant to surprise, but so often they are the same surprising questions you've heard four times already that week. Still, the DJs are nice enough to let you on their morning show to promote your music or concert, so you're happy to play along.

"Fave hockey team?"

"Habs."

DJ is confused, as he is sure I was a Leafs fan, but continues, excitedly.

"What CD would you chose to listen to for the rest of your life?'

"*Bob Marley's Greatest Hits.*"

DJ is surprised again, as he never assumed I'd like reggae, but again he forges ahead.

"If you could have dinner with anyone in history, alive or dead, who would it be?"

"The Fella with the Vinegar Sponge."

DJ usually turns his head like a dog when asked if it wants a snack. He tries so very hard to stick to the plot, but the curveball he's been thrown is just too whacky.

"Excuse me, what?"

I repeat, straight-faced.

"The Fella with the Vinegar Sponge."

DJ wants to know more about this most curious response, but I know he's got to hit the 9 a.m. news and doesn't have time for a theological discussion, so I usually say politely, "He's the most interesting fella in the Bible, I think. Look him up after your shift." DJ then finishes with a "hot dogs or hamburgers?" question, and I'm out the door. I usually glance back to see him either staring at me like I am the strangest thing he's ever encountered, or I see him already googling "bible man with the vinegar spo . . ."

——

Since I was a child, I have been fascinated with all things religious, especially Catholic things, as that was my stripe. Religion defined the very geography of my town—Petty Harbour was divided by a river separating a school, church, store and fish plant for the town's Catholic community, and a school, church, store and fish plant on the other side for the Protestant community. Born into a very Catholic family, I served as an altar boy for a number of years, and as a young man, I did a religious studies degree at Memorial University.

I have written before about my utter bewilderment with the Catholic notion of transubstantiation, where the body and blood of Christ defies physics and actually—not spiritually or ceremonially—becomes a thin wafer of communal bread. What I found most curious about this belief was that almost no adults I knew were aware of this, assuming instead that Christ's body was simply represented in the host, not the actual host. When I mentioned this discrepancy to the parish priest, he insisted I stay quiet about it and not ask too many questions. How odd, I figured, to be told to stop asking questions about something you were told was very important. I have been interested in it ever since.

The first I heard of the man with the vinegar sponge was while standing on the altar in a white sutan, sometime between ages ten and thirteen. The gospel that Sunday must have been from either Mark 15 or Matthew 27, as these chapters contain the two most direct references to the gent who would fascinate me to this day.

Father O'Brien noted in his homily: "And there on the cross, our beloved saviour Jesus Christ suffered for our sins. All the while being mocked by Roman soldiers who had the cruellest of intentions and would not even give Jesus a drink of water on his deathbed. Yes, that is how much punishment our Lord endured for us at the hands of those who would offer a dying man vinegar for water and laugh at him as he died!" I saw Mary Mulloney in the congregation bless herself, then bow her shaking head and draw her cardigan closer together high at the chest, the unspoken sign for "disgusted worry" for Newfoundland ladies of a certain vintage.

I can't say for sure this was the first time my young Petty Harbor Catholic self uttered the phrase, "What the f—k?" But there, on the red-carpet altar at St. Joseph's parish, is most definitely my earliest memory of uttering this phrase, even if under my breath.

I missed several altar boy service cues at the tail end of the mass, distracted by what seemed to be the most random act of mischief or cruelty I'd ever heard of in my young life.

I was late serving the wine and water at the Preparation of the Gifts because my mind raced with the question, "Where did that fella get the vinegar?" I almost dropped the host plate while walking to Father O'Brien and wondering, "Did he bring the vinegar, or was it just around by some weird accident?" By the time I was to lift the Baptismal candle and join the Closing Procession, I was tumbling down a mind hole. My mom kicked into the intro of "Sing to the Mountains" on the old church organ, but I could not bring myself to sing. "If he brought the vinegar, which I suppose he must have, did he do so because he wanted to mock Jesus? 'Cause if so, that is particularly malicious." And I almost tripped, knocking down the whole parade domino-style, as the most horrific thought yet occurred to me: "Sweet Holy Jesus, did he bring the friggin' vinegar every day? For everyone getting crucified? For his own private jollies?" Then, for the second time, "What the f—k?"

Ever since that day, the fellow with the vinegar sponge remains one of the people I would most like to talk with. How I might delicately broach the subject during a dinner conversation with him, however, remains a question mark.

"Welcome, welcome, man, thanks so much for joining me. So cool, isn't it, this new app that lets living people pull dinner guests out of heaven or hell or purgatory or wherever you've been hanging out—no judgment, by the way. I hope you like the fish my mom fried for us. My uncle caught it only this morning, so it's pretty fresh. You shouldn't need hardly any vinegar on it . . . unless you loves vinegar?"

After the appetizers, would I get more specific?

"So, Stephaton [as he is sometimes called], you spent most of your life as a Roman soldier, is that right? Ah. Cool, cool. So, you must have been at a few of those crucifixions, I suppose?"

Maybe after the main course while waiting for dessert I would probe a bit more?

"Man, that uniform is still sharp-looking. I suppose the Roman Army gave you that and your weapons, did they? Yeah, that spear and sword are badass, b'y. Did they provide you with anything else? Like your lunch, maybe? Or did you have to brown bag it to the crucifixions? Bring a sand-wich? A bottle of wine, perhaps . . . ?"

But by the time the apple pie was done, and our dinner date coming to a close, I suspect a lifetime of pent-up questions would simply spill out, supper-table etiquette be damned.

"Bud, you got to tell me—what the f—k with the vine-gar? Times were different, I get it. But did you carry it all the time? Did you wake up each day before the wife and kids and giggle as you snuck it out the pantry and poured it into your water bottle? Were you trying to look cool in front of the other soldiers? Trying to top that popular guy who brought a rotten egg to hurl at the dying fella during last week's crucifixion? Were you home one night stewing, 'Shag you, Longinus, and your friggin' side spear. You think that's the something, you big show-off! Well, here's the most insulting finisher yet—vinegar for water!'"

By now, I imagine the poor fella would be trying to find the door.

"Did you get high fives in the Roman Soldier lunchroom later that day as the legend started making the rounds? Did they stand and slow clap as you entered? Did Longinus run over with arms spread and proclaim, 'Dude, vinegar! That's next level! You're a star, man!' Or was it the kind of thing you always wanted to do but instantly regretted? You know, like kissing your girlfriend's sister?"

As the poor embattled fella ran down the walkway, I'd still be shouting,

"I'm sorry, but I have to ask—did someone make you drink vinegar when you were small? Did someone hurt you? It's okay to say, you know. This is a safe space!"

One of the last things he'd hear as he rounded the corner for Duckworth Street, his spear dragging behind him on the sidewalk and sword banging awkwardly against his surprisingly feminine skirt and exposed knees, might be me politely trying to woo him back for an after-supper nightcap.

"We all do stupid things we regret, man—no judgment! Come back, come back!"

And finally,

"Can I offer you something to drink?!"

The Duke is a British pub. There are more Irish pubs in St. John's, and I do love both types. Traditional Irish ones tend to have live music onstage or an informal tunes session in the corner, while the British ones almost never have live music and almost always have food.

I've loved pubs since I first stepped into one in St. John's in the mid-1980s. I'd never seen the likes of it. People often think of Newfoundland as having a pub culture, but it's not true. The fishing towns of rural Newfoundland are dotted with Legions and clubs for dances and weddings but very few pubs. Pubs are a Townie thing in Newfoundland. And this one is my favourite.

A British pub. Reminds me of my first time in Britain. Or anywhere, for that matter.

THE FRENCHMAN & THE BIRD

"GIVE ME BACK my money or I'll take your bird and you'll never see it again." I was serious too.

Standing at the edge of the Thames under Westminster Bridge, Big Ben pounding noon in the cold hard light of day, I was face to face with a conman who had all but successfully scammed me out of my last twenty-pound note. He had my money. But I had his bird.

"Give me my money!" I shouted, my nineteen-year-old Petty Harbour voice echoing off the stone walkways and bouncing off the bridge as a small lunchtime crowd of locals gathered to witness the standoff.

"Please, monsieur, do not 'urt my bird." Oh, he was definitely playing up his "gentle old Frenchman" accent, the fraudster. I stared him down. I was doing God's work. "My money back, or the bird is coming with me."

———

It was spring 1989 and I had taken my first-ever plane off Newfoundland. My brother, Bernie, was doing a three-month internship at Memorial University's extension campus in a town in Essex called Harlow, just outside of London, and I was excited to ride his coattails yet again. Yes, my first trip from Newfoundland was from Petty Harbour to London, England. The first and only city I had ever walked in was tiny, quaint, homogeneously settled St. John's, where every face is exactly the same shape and shade. The second was a city of almost ten million, with practically every type and race and size and shape of human on Earth.

I boarded the plane just after 9:30 p.m. and took my seat. I did not sleep a wink during the flight, as I was so excited to not only leave my rock in the middle of the ocean but also to visit my older brother in one of the greatest cities of human history. I suppose I also wanted to prove to myself, and anyone else who cared, that I was capable of living happily outside the hilly and watery boundaries of Petty Harbour. I spent the entire flight imagining myself wandering the streets of London and Dublin without a hitch. With the endurance only youth can muster, I wasn't the slightest bit tired when the Air Canada plane landed at London's Heathrow Airport the next morning. After we disembarked, I walked through the airport halls for what felt like an eternity—without question, the longest interior trek of my life. In the time I walked from the plane to the airport exit, I could have walked across Petty Harbour ten times.

Bernie was waiting for me, having taken an early train from Harlow to meet me. I wanted to step outside and place my foot on British soil for the first time, but Bernie insisted that we go immediately downstairs to the subway and head into Central London.

"Jesus, Alan, b'y, we can't have the first thing you see outside of Newfoundland be the parking lot at Heathrow. That's just not right."

We descended what felt like an impossible number of stories below ground level and boarded a subway train. This was my first-ever time on a subway, or any train, for that matter. Come to think of it, it was the first time I had ever been this far underground. Already this trip was an eye-opener.

The train doors closed and we took seats close to a window. We rolled through the dark tunnel, and a moment or two later I squinted as a blast of sunlight shone through the windows. When my vision cleared, I saw for the first time I was somewhere other than Newfoundland. I was in England.

One of the first things I recognized was a British taxi driving close to us on the highway beside the railway tracks. The cab looked exactly like it did on TV, with the steering wheel on the wrong side and oversized windows, and I spotted a chubby English fella talking inside. I was surprised to see fields in the distance, and even more surprised to see fields with cows grazing them. Not sure why, but it never occurred to me there might be livestock around London. I figured it would be all Oliver Twists and Sherlock Holmes and James Bonds and Jack the Rippers, I suppose.

"Jesus Christ!" I jumped out of my seat like someone had poured boiling water over my crotch. A train headed in the opposite direction sped past us, only inches from my face.

"Trains goes both ways, Alan, b'y. And there's more than one track, you know," Bernie muttered. These two facts had never once occurred to me. So much for being cool as a cucumber outside of Petty Harbour.

As the train rolled closer to the city, it again dove underground. When the subway finally rolled into Piccadilly Circus, Bernie said, "This is us." I grabbed my knapsack and followed him through another myriad of hallways. Along the way, we passed a Hare Krishna monk who was busking, not by chanting or singing, but instead by funk-slapping a bass guitar while kicking out eight notes on a shaker attached to his right ankle and playing two and four backbeats with his left ankle. His head was as bare as his feet. It remains one of the coolest musical acts of coordination I have ever seen.

I was so mesmerized by the bass-playing monk that I did not notice we had stepped onto an escalator. I had been on the escalator at the Avalon Mall and the Village Mall in Newfoundland many times, but as I turned my head and looked up, my mouth dropped. Before me lay what appeared to be a kilometre and a half of escalator.

"Holy shit," I said a little too loud, as some of the other riders turned to see what had startled me. "This is the biggest friggin' escalator I ever saw. Must be four hundred people on it."

"F—k, yes." Bernie was excited for my excitement, and he turned his head to enjoy how freaked out I was.

"Is this safe?" I whispered.

"F—k, no." I couldn't tell if Bernie was kidding or not.

We walked among what I can only describe as an unsafe amount of people, all pushing towards what I hoped was the exit as a growing glint of sunlight reflected off the archway ceiling.

When we were finally reborn onto the sidewalk, I was undeniably in London, England. Car horns blared from the wrong side of the road, large-hatted bobbies walked in pairs and every other stride seemed to require me to scoot around a stand selling newspapers that all seemed to be about some soccer fella and a brothel.

In just a few steps, we were in Trafalgar Square.

"Have a seat under this lion and I'll get us a coffee." Bernie disappeared into the crowd.

I estimated that in every blink of my eyes, I saw more people per glance than the entire population of Petty Harbour. I estimated that in the ten minutes that Bernie was away, I saw more people than I had in the entire nineteen years of my life combined.

What I wanted to do, more than anything, was randomly stop people. Just grab every hundredth person by the arm and say, "Excuse me, I am just curious. Where are you going?" I could not fathom how this many people could have somewhere to go at the same time.

I was almost twenty years old, but in a big city at rush hour for the first time. I had just flown on a plane for the first time and sat on a subway for the first time. It was the first time I ever saw traffic. The first time I saw more than a couple races of people in one glance. Soon, I had my first kiss from a Spanish man when Bernie's pal Eduardo greeted me. An Italian pal of his would cook me my first spicy chicken dish, which numbed me for a day and a half. I had my first taste of curry. My first Cornish pasty. My first jacket spud covered in butter and beans from a sidewalk cart.

"I thought the food was supposed to be bad here?!" I was in culinary heaven.

So many firsts would come so quickly. I was here to come of age and getting the crash course.

I also had my first pint of Guinness, which I loved immediately. But Bernie swore it would be even better when we got to Dublin, which we did a night or two later.

We took a train to Holyhead, and from there ferried to Ireland, a mecca of sorts for us two fellas from the southern shore of Newfoundland, known as the Irish Loop. There were many firsts in the Mother Country, including my first pint of Guinness in Dublin, which was everything Bernie said it would be and maybe the best drink I've had to this day. That night led to Saturday morning, when we took a bus to Glendalough, my first trip to an ancient monastery, and then that day led to a night out in the clubs of Dublin and my first time saying, "Perhaps we better call it a night" to a girl after she whispered outside her door, "Shh, don't wake me Da. He gets pissed when I brings fellas home." This led to my first sprint through the streets of Dublin to avoid potential injury, which led to my first time getting lost in Dublin, or anywhere else, for that matter.

The Sunday church bells were ringing by the time I finally found my way back to the hostel. I walked through the door just as they were kicking Bernie out for staying past our reservation time.

"I can't leave without my bro—" Then he saw me rounding the corner. "Jesus, Alan, where the f—k were you?" Bernie was actually worried about me and didn't mind saying so.

That was a first too, I figured.

We followed through on our genius plan to take the night ferry back to England so we would not have to rent a room. I had only twenty pounds left in my wallet, so grabbing a nap on the boat was a good enough plan for me.

However, there would be no sleep on that journey. Onboard, we met a group of Irish fellas who tried so hard to convince us we should carry their long, suspicious-looking tubes across British Customs.

"Ye crowd are lovely Canadians," one fella said. His *crowd* sounded more like *cried*. "They won't check anything ye got."

"What's in them?" I asked apprehensively, figuring he would say flowers for Mom or something clearly untrue.

"Rifles," he said, straight-faced. "Hunting rifles. You know. And poles for fishing too."

As Buddy tried to convince us, Bernie yanked me by the Canadian-flag bandana I had tied to a belt loop on my jeans. I'd worn this the whole trip but had never done so before. I figured I should look more worldly if I was to actually be more worldly. On any previous occasion, Bernie would have gave me the gears about such an obvious fashion ploy to look something I was not, just as I would have done to him. But he never mentioned it. Another first. I guess we were both eager to come of age in our own way.

In any case, he grabbed me by the flag bandana and we spent the next several hours walking through the midnight ferry ride to avoid getting charged with conspiracy to transport weapons across an international border. At about three in the morning, we boarded a horribly stinky bus for a five-hour bumpy ride back to London. It took eight and a half hours.

I had not slept since Thursday night when we arrived back in London late Monday morning. We stumbled out of the bus station and zombie-walked past St. James Park towards the Houses of Parliament. Bernie pointed to a side street at the end of the park.

"Prime Minster lives down there, if you wants to see it."

"Nope." All I wanted was a bunk. We continued heading towards the train station that would take us back to Harlow.

But as we walked past Big Ben and under Westminster Bridge to the Thames path, a timid yet tempting voice spoke to me from the shadows.

"Une photo avec l'oiseau? A picture with the bird?"

"What?" I could not even muster politeness.

A small, somewhat frail old Frenchman stepped into the noon light. He looked like a mix between Fagin from *Oliver Twist* and Geppetto, the old fella who built Pinocchio. On his shoulder sat a tiny red and yellow bird who calmly and quietly perched, appearing to await direction from its trainer. Fagin's thick accent was heavier than Québécois, but he spoke so slowly that it was not hard to understand him at all.

"A souvenir to take 'ome, no? Just vingt pounds, and I mail you picture with you and bird and clock tower too."

"Vingt pounds?" I was so sleep-deprived that I could not manage to comprehend a foreign language and currency at the same time. He pointed to my wallet, and in my haze, I took it out. He was so gentle and kind that I could only assume I should do what he said. My wallet unfolded and he pointed to the one and only note in there, a twenty-pounder, and continued quietly and peacefully inquiring like a massage therapist might as you were registering at a spa.

"You are from Canada?" he said, pointing to the maple leaf on my bandana. "Beautiful country. What is your name and address?"

I was transfixed by the bird's gaze. He stared at me with one unblinking eye, his head turned in profile. I was so hypnotized by this perfect little creature that I did not notice myself answering the Frenchman.

"Alan Doyle Box 45 Petty Harbour Newfoundland Canada."

"Ah, Terre-Neuve. Great friends to us in the War." Already under the hypnotic spell of the bird, I was so surprised that he knew about Newfoundland that I didn't notice he had reached into my wallet and taken the twenty-pound note.

"I will send you two pictures for nice souvenir." He held the note up to me and pocketed it, then placed the little bird on my shoulder.

"Click." The camera sounded particularly old. The bird jumped from my shoulder to my head.

"Click." With that second sound, the bird jumped back on the Frenchman's shoulder.

"Merci," he said and turned back to the crowd.

Perhaps it was his departure, or perhaps it was the fact that I was finally unlocked from the bird's mesmerizing gaze. But in a second the spell I had been under was broken. I shook my head a couple of times and turned to see Bernie looking at me bewildered.

"What was that all about?" He craned his neck to keep an eye on the old man, who was quickly disappearing into the lunch crowd on the banks of the Thames.

"Oh, some old fella said he'll send me pictures with the bird." I was still not really awake.

"Did you just give him your last twenty pounds for that? You knows he's not gonna send you anything. There's probably not even film in the camera." I did not want to believe what was blatantly obvious to my smarter, wiser and well-travelled older brother.

"He took my address, though." As I spoke, I saw the scam I had just fell for.

"Did he write it down?" Again, Bernie with the smart question. I just hung my head.

"I don't know, to be honest."

"You just lost twenty pounds." Bernie turned to continue our walk down to the train station, amused by my foolishness but completely prepared to let it all go.

"No f—king way." I had not even finished speaking as I turned back to the noon crowd and ran to catch the cheater.

"What are you doing?!" Bernie shouted.

"I am getting my money back!" I pushed my way through the crowd like I was in a spy movie searching for the detonator as the seconds counted down.

I found the bird man a short distance down the river, trying to scam two more innocent people in his perfectly convincing trickster way. I was having none of it. I did not leave Petty Harbor and the island of Newfoundland for the very first time to be had by this thief. This trip was my coming-of-age party. I came here to prove I was a smart and worldly person, not to be shown that I could be taken by this scammer and his seductress bird.

"Hey! Give me my money back!" I shouted so that his

next victims and all those around could hear me. Why not broadcast this interaction for all to see and hear, I figured. I would be the hero of this story.

"Pardon?" the old man said. He turned to me, and as he did, I lifted the yellow and red bird from his shoulder and held it in my hands.

"Give me back my money or I'll take your bird and you'll never see it again."

"Please, monsieur, do not 'urt my bird." French Fagin looked to be caving now as he reached for his pocket.

"My money back, or the bird is coming with me." My Bayman hands clenched his bird like a vise.

By now Bernie had caught up and was startled to see the standoff I had created. He pushed his way through the circle of people.

"Jesus, Alan. What are you at?"

The Frenchman handed me the twenty and I figured I was about to deliver my hero line of the movie in my mind. I had finally defeated the bad guy and would deliver the catchphrase that would most definitely make it to the trailer.

"Nothing now, Bernie. Nothing now." I held my twenty-pound note in one hand and released the bird with my other. It jumped back onto the shoulder of the Frenchman.

As I strode away with a newfound swagger, I could not understand why so few—well, no one in fact—applauded.

———

We had another few days in Harlow and the greater London area, and I learned so much and had still more firsts than I can tell in this story.

What I can tell you is that about three weeks later I walked into our kitchen back in Petty Harbour to the familiar smells of Mom's bread baking in the oven.

"Bread day! Yes, b'y!" I said loud enough to announce my presence.

"Yes, Alan honey, that'll be out in ten minutes or so and you can have it hot." Mom's voice, music to my ears as ever.

"Wicked." I sat in my usual spot at the kitchen table while Mom stirred a pot of beef stew on the stove. A boiler of white potatoes sat idle next to her. Home.

"Oh, Alan honey, a letter came in the mail for you this morning." As I looked up from the potato boiler, Mom stood holding a well-travelled, faded white envelope with what was clearly a Royal Mail stamp. "Who's that from?"

I had no idea and hurriedly opened it.

The next thing I heard was Mom's voice.

"Jesus, Alan honey, what is it? You looks like someone who just saw a ghost."

I did not answer. The shame shut me up.

I stared at two colour photos of me on the edge of the Thames under the Big Ben clock tower. A lovely yellow and red bird was on my shoulder in one photo, and on my head in the other.

I have been to London many times since, and whenever possible, I walk down to that spot under the bridge by Big

Ben and the Houses of Parliament. It remains a popular busking location. I never found that old Frenchman again, but every time I stroll through it I get a surprised and delighted "Cheers" from a singer or player with a hat with a few scattered coins before him as I lay a twenty-pound note and pause for what must look to be a little too long before I nod and stroll on.

Bernie loves the corner seat at the Duke as much as me. I'm afraid to get up to go to the men's room 'cause this spot will be long gone when I gets back. We've done a lot together over the years. Me following him. Him following me. And both of us just trying to figure it all out together.

"You'd sooner piss yourself as give up that seat." Bernie tips his pint with respect, as he'd be as protective of this stool as I am being now. He offers, "That's a hard-earned throne."

I tip my glass back.

He knows I'm saying "Amen" as much as "Cheers."

The Basement

MY BROTHER, BERNIE, is around two years older than me but looks quite a bit younger. New friends are often surprised to learn that I am not the senior of us. When asked about this, Bernie usually says, "Yes, I do look younger than my brother, even though I was a couple of grades ahead of him in school. But you've got to remember one important fact. I've only been awake half as long as Alan."

My brother and I have followed each other around the world over the years, with me chasing him to London or Texas, and him chasing me to Berlin or Los Angeles. We've had our spats like any brothers do, but mostly we get along great. Our bond was forged cutting wood and digging holes and whatever other task we were assigned as teens in Petty Harbour. We don't agree on everything, but we definitely agree that our father's favourite pastime was getting us out of bed to do work.

Our father loved to make work for me and my brother, and he often did so without much consideration for how sensible the labour plan was. I suspect it gave him great satisfaction to have us at something, mattering little to him whether it was the best or worst way to get the job done so long as we were not lying in bed or watching TV.

Carrying firewood, for example, from the sled to the side of the house made total sense and was done willingly and even with a smile at times. But carrying wood back to the sled, moving it to the other side of the yard for two weeks only to move it back, was done begrudgingly. Stacking the firewood for a month, then unstacking it to split it up and then restacking it also seemed poorly planned. Especially considering much of that same pile of wood would shortly be unpiled and split into smaller splits to light the fire.

By the time the wood was about to be burned, we almost felt bad. We'd spent so much time together, we were like old friends.

"I'm after holding this piece of wood at least a couple of dozen times." I mock sniffed. "I'm after undressing it, and travelling with it. I'm after tossing it playfully in the air and resting my head on it as we took a romantic sled ride in the snow. I have touched it inside and out. Friggin' sin that I am made to kill and burn one of my most intimate friends."

Every Saturday morning, Dad woke Bernie and me for one job or the other. The odd day when there was neither school nor Mass to contend with, we dreamt of sleeping in our tiny rickety bunkbeds till late morning or even till noon, as we'd heard some of our friends did. But it never happened. If there was not something that needed to be done immediately, Dad would find something less than pressing. Not unlike restacking the wood for the umpteenth time.

We wondered why this constant menial job assignment dogged us so consistently.

We cleared it all up one Saturday morning during a minor protest when Dad woke us to help him pull nails out of old clapboard he'd gotten for free. You see, this kind of thing happened all the time in Petty Harbour. Nothing was ever wasted. When one man tore down a shed, another man got old naily lumber to burn in the fire. Rural Newfoundland gents of my dad's vintage are sickened by the thought of throwing away decent material and giddy at the thought of getting something for free, no matter how much time and effort is expended to get it.

"Dad would drive to Corner Brook to get twenty dollars' worth of free two-by-fours," I whined as we rolled out of our Saturday morning bunks at seven thirty.

This nail-pulling needed to be done eventually. But it was definitely not time-sensitive as far as we were concerned. This seemed way less important than sleeping in to Bernie and me, and though we knew better than to complain, we could not hold it in.

I put the simplest question to my father.

"Dad, are you afraid to let us sleep in, or what?"

And I got the simplest answer.

"Yes, b'y. Yes, I am."

And that was the truth. He was afraid of his boys being lazy. He wanted them active and productive. He was not too concerned about what they were doing, as long as they were doing something. He was not afraid of his boys being musicians or doctors, fishermen or farmers, policemen or teachers, soldiers or spies, or priests or even thieves, it seemed. But he was terrified of them becoming lazy.

Mom shared this fear, and she often drove my older sister just as hard with house chores like dishwashing, laundry, bed-making, sewing and other traditional women's work such as minding my baby sister.

In a house with few regulations, The Father and The Mother shared one common constant unbreakable rule.

The Only Thing You Can't Do Is Nothing.

Dad proclaimed two things at the toast-and-tea breakfast table one Saturday morning. The first was not a big deal to us boys. The second one most certainly was.

"We got to get a bigger wood furnace," my father proclaimed. "It will heat the house better with less wood."

We were happy to hear that this new furnace would require less wood. Perhaps we might actually get to sleep in the odd Saturday morning.

And then Dad added, "But it will be big and will have to go in the basement."

Now this was a very big deal to Bernie and me for one practical reason: we did not have a basement.

The house that we lived in was perched on a rocky hill. This was true for most houses in Petty Harbour, and like most of those houses, ours was very small. It had a tiny kitchen and living room on the main floor and three tiny bedrooms upstairs, with a small washroom at the end of the hall. Dad and several other men in the town had built the house themselves, partly from wood they'd cut and dragged on their backs from the hills and taken to be milled. Despite the fact that they weren't carpenters by trade, the house was solid. It kept our family warm and mostly dry, and survived many a rough night in wind, rain and snow. There was not a straight line or flush wall or ninety-degree angle in the place, but it served us well and was something to be proud of.

But it did not have a basement.

Our house had been laid on a perimeter of concrete that outlined the house's footprint. The concrete was poured in forms two to three feet high, depending on the height of the bedrock on which they stood. Within the concrete perimeter, the house was built over the mud and rock and boulders that were common all over town. When completed, there lay a crawl space under the house that was as high as three feet in a few places but ranged mostly between one and two feet. A hatch in the porch provided access.

At the tea-and-toast breakfast table, it was Kim who spoke first.

"But we don't have a basement."

"Yes, but the boys will dig one. It'll only take a while." Dad seemed delighted by this prospect. Bernie and I did not.

"Dad, that's impossible." I almost laid down my toast.

"No, I don't think it is impossible," Dad said. "It might be hard. But not impossible. We'll cut a window on the back side and start there. We can shovel the dirt mud out through the window. Same with the smaller rocks."

"What about the bigger ones?" Bernie said. He was an engineer long before he went to university and got a piece of paper to confirm it.

"We'll have to beat them up with a sledgehammer till they are small enough to pass through the window, I s'pose." Dad folded a thick-cut slice of Mom's white bread and jammed the works into his mouth, chasing it with hot tea.

And that was the end of the discussion. We were going to dig a basement under a house that had already been built. "This is the most poorly planned job ever," I figured, but there was no sense bringing that up now.

When me and my brother got home from school on Friday afternoon, there was a man I recognized from the Protestant side of the harbour at the back of the house. This man worked in construction somewhere up the shore and had access to real power tools and other cool stuff. He and Dad were crouched by the concrete foundation wall with a large gas-powered saw with a blade as big as I had ever seen. They had cut three sides of a rectangular window, and the cuts had left dark grey lines in the concrete.

I wondered if the hole was too small, but Dad said that he had gotten a free window from Eddie on the garbage truck, so that was the window they were using. They would install the window once the basement was complete, and in the meantime, they'd nail a piece of old plywood over the opening to keep the cats and rats out at nights.

When he had finished the last cut, the Protestant fella cleverly tapped one side of the concrete block and the other side popped out. He and Dad grabbed it, pulled it out, and there it was. A window into the basement.

This was like having a portal to a new world. A bridge across the river. I had seen the crawl space from the hatch above but had never truly seen under our house. I dropped to my knees and stuck my head into the blackness of the opening. When my eyes adjusted, the full state of the task ahead was revealed for the first time.

A ladder in the crawl space led to the only place where a grown-up could crouch. There, in about three feet of head clearance, was where our old oil furnace had been installed years before. It was possible, but difficult, to climb down the ladder and service the furnace when required. Which was often, as the furnace constantly broke or needed to be primed again.

This was the only accessible part of the entire as-yet-to-built basement. The rest was an expanse of black dirt, mud and rocks that stretched as far as the little daylight seeping through the opening would allow me to see. Me and my brother would have to dig a hole as big as the floor of our entire house, six to eight feet deep, with picks and shovels and sledgehammers, and somehow get all the fill out through the small rectangular window about the size of a bread box.

The next morning, Dad burst into our room and knocked as hard as he could on the footboard of our bunkbeds. This was his preferred method of waking us up.

"Let's go. We got a hole to dig." He said it like we'd have the job done by lunchtime.

We went down the hatch in the porch and, one by one, squatted in the space next to the oil furnace.

"First thing, we got to make a path to the window." Dad was obviously eager.

We figured the best place to start digging was the furnace area where we were crouching, so that we'd have a space with enough room to stand. With no access to the window, we'd have to carry the dirt and rocks up the ladder in buckets. We quickly got a chain going with Bernie shovelling, Dad carrying the filled buckets up the ladder and me carrying the buckets out back of the house and dumping them over the bank.

In an hour or so, there was enough room for one person to stand, and by lunchtime all three of us could stand. We were making serious progress by the time my sister Kim came to the hatch and shouted that the soup and sandwiches were ready.

Over lunch, the three of us bragged about our strength and how we would have this licked by suppertime. We figured by next weekend we would be watching the hockey game downstairs in our new family room, or whatever the room was called where well-to-do families watched TV.

With our bellies filled with canned tomato soup and bologna sandwiches, and our hearts filled with hope, we three set back down to the job at hand. We decided to follow the outline of the crawl space's concrete perimeter until we had dug a path to the new window tall enough for everyone to stand. Then we could use the window for dirt and rock disposal and be done with the tiresome lugging of buckets.

We started down the would-be path, with shovels and picks ready at the hip. And then it happened. My shovel broke the dirt and hit a massive boulder. In truth, it was inevitable, but the progress of the early morning and the hope we shared over the sandwiches had filled us with a false sense of what lay ahead. The boulder looked to be almost as big as the chair in the living room, the one where Mom would sit and knit.

The boulder would not move. We dug around it to get a sense of its full size and then started at it with sledgehammers. By suppertime, we had taken one corner off, about as big as a microwave oven. It would take us two more full Saturdays of hacking and pounding and picking till the heart of the boulder finally split and we could build a pulley system to haul the parts up the ladder and out the back door. After two weeks of after-schools and Saturdays, we boys finally made it to the window.

We figured life would be happy and gay after disposing of the bucket requirement. We so happily dug down below the window and slid the dirt and rocks out through the opening. But slowly we began to discover another obstacle we should have seen coming. The more we happily dug under the window, the higher we would have to lift each shovelful to get it out the opening.

We had reached what we'd envisioned would be the place where things got easier. Now, we saw that things would be as hard as ever.

One Saturday morning, I went down the ladder and noticed I had forgotten the day before to nail the piece of plywood over the window hole. I wondered if a cat or a rat may have gotten in, but didn't see any evidence of one. It was not until I reached for the shovel that a shadow and a scurrying sound caught my attention. It was coming from the ceiling.

I pressed my back against the concrete wall under the window and lay perfectly still, hoping to get a look at whatever it was. I stared into the dark corners of the joists, wires and rusty ductwork over my head. Then, it dropped from the ceiling into the mud.

The biggest mink I had ever seen reared up on its hind legs.

The fella was not pleased to have his way to the window blocked by anyone, and he hissed at me. I was too scared to make a sound, as I knew from growing up on the banks of a river that a cornered mink would attack anyone who threatened him. So I just lay there as flat as could be and tried to give Mr. Mink a path to get out. Mr. Mink hissed a few more times, spat something and then bolted. As quickly as anything I had ever seen, the mink ran over my chest and leaped out the window.

I was still speechless when Bernie came down the ladder. "What's your problem?" he asked.

"Frig friggin' mink," I stuttered. "Got in. Got out over me shirt." I pointed to the mud tracks on my chest.

"Bullshit. You're just trying to get out of havin' to shovel today." Bernie tossed me a shovel and that was that. We were back to basement digging. A tedious back-breaking task made worse now by the constant fear of being attacked by some feral beast.

We pressed on, and with the aid of a single light bulb on an old extension cord, we found we could work later in the evenings and after suppers. Bernie rigged a small ramp out of an old pallet to make the hoisting of the heavy stones easier. We zigzagged our way around the largest boulders and removed all the dirt through the tiny window. To look down through the hatch now was to see what resembled an archaeological dig. Paths beaten into the mud, twisting around boulders. Two ants working in a farm oblivious to all else but the task at hand. As we got closer to clearing all the dirt that could be removed, we began to lobby Dad for a jackhammer to beat up the last of the largest rocks. We figured we could get one off the Protestant fella and as a reward for our weeks and months of hard labour underground. Dad was not easily swayed to such luxuries as jackhammers, but he reluctantly agreed.

As it turned out, the Protestant fella would come the following Saturday and beat up the remaining boulders with a jackhammer himself. Good thing, as I could hardly lift it and Bernie nearly took his foot off within the first five minutes of using it.

When the boulders were beat to bits the size of footballs, the man left with his gear and Bernie and I looked over a mound of rock that seemed to take up more space than the boulders themselves did. For the next few weeks, on Saturdays and after-schools and evenings, we lugged rocks to the window and chucked them as far as we could.

We had been leaving a ceremonial rock for the final throw. The rock we chose was a rock I had cut my hand on and Bernie had nearly crippled himself trying to jackhammer open. It could very well have been the same one the mink leapt from to escape without having to disfigure me.

We did everything else first, as we wanted the flicking of this rock from the new floor of our house to be cause for great celebration. When the time finally arrived, we gathered everyone together. Bernie and I picked up the rock together and walked to the window. On the count of three from the whole family, we chucked it out the window and over the bank. It had now been seven months since Dad had told us about his plan to put a new wood furnace in the basement.

Everyone cheered and applauded. Mom hugged us and told us we could go to the take-out and have whatever we wanted. Then we climbed the ladder to start the evening's party.

I was last to leave and paused for moment to look around. Before me was the hole we'd been digging, shovel and pick marks etched into rock, mud on tools and boots and dust settling on bloody gloves with holes in the palms.

But I did not see this at all.

I saw a room. It was a room with mud floors and walls made of concrete and rock. A room with a ceiling of busted pipes and wires and rusty ductwork that led to a furnace that had not worked properly in years. A room that smelled of oil and stagnant water. A room that could very well have a family or two of feral minks or rats or cats living in the rafters.

But it was a room. It was a room that would get floor joists and Gyproc walls. A place where a wood-fired furnace would be easily accessible by stairs. I heard Mom say she wanted to put a real washer and dryer down there so she would not have to fold clothes on the muddy porch.

It was a room we had carved from a space that had not even existed before Dad woke us that Saturday morning. It was our room.

And with this one look, it became my favourite room. It still is.

Rhonda runs the big hotel in town. In most other cities she would be considered the life of the party, but here she can barely get a word in, which suits her fine, I think. She loves to surround herself with loud artist types whose joie de vivre offers a sharp contrast to the more structured and conservative business world of managing a branch of a world-wide hotel.

When she does get to speak, she often brings a tale of someone they had to oust from a room for making too much noise, or some fella caught shagging someone he was not supposed to and seen running in his drawers out the door and up Barters Hill, chased by an angry fella with a hockey stick.

I always love her stories and, in good pub chat form, love how they lead to my own.

ONE SPRING A few years ago, our relationship with some Danish promoters and managers paid off and GBS was offered the support slot for the well-weathered but newly reinvented Scottish Celtic rock band Runrig. A decade or so previous, Runrig was a top draw in several countries in Europe with their big 1980s rock meets traditional Celtic sound. Cape Breton native and old friend of ours, Bruce Guthro, had recently been hired to replace the band's original singer, and though he's too humble to admit it, I'm sure he put in a good word for us to open the tour.

His collaboration with the Scottish icons was working out really well. They had recently released the CD *The Stamping Ground* and would have their first charting hit in Europe in years. The tour was to start in April on the Isle of

Skye in Portree, Scotland, and roll in two legs through the UK and across the sea into Denmark and Germany, two of the band's biggest support bases on the mainland.

We would get to play a thirty-minute opening set each night and then blast to the merch table to sign and sell as many CDs as possible since our fee for the set was zero. This was and probably still is quite common in European touring, where the support act does the tour for merch sales and promotion alone. Runrig actually stepped up to the plate heartily and offered us catered suppers each night from their travelling chefs and a hearty backstage rider, which was quite unusual at the time. They remain some of the kindest people we've ever met on the road.

It would be a long tour for us, as we did not have enough money to fly everyone home for the ten-day break in the middle of the tour, so we'd be on the road for almost eight weeks straight. We planned to occupy the ten-day downtime with our own pub gigs while waiting for the big tour to kick back in. (If memory serves me correctly, those gigs never really materialized, so some of us did the responsible thing any travelling band guys in their youth would do: we went to Amsterdam for four days. Very productive.)

Financing the Runrig tour would prove very tricky. We would be a touring party of six people, and since we'd recently made the jump of staying in separate hotel rooms, there was no looking back. So we needed six hotel rooms, as well as transport for six people and equipment. I believe we trashed the idea of a per diem of any kind, our justification being that the hotels provided a breakfast that we'd make sure to eat as much of as we could, while Runrig were providing dinner.

As another cost-saving measure, we struck up a deal with a hotel chain in the UK, the Red Roof Inn. They had locations in many of the cities we were to play, and they'd offer us a reduced rate if we booked as many room nights as possible with them. We agreed and were pleasantly surprised upon arrival at the first one in Scotland that the hotel was a brand-new, clean, Euro-Ikea-ish styled place, the sort with lots of metal-legged furniture and laminated birchy wood tops and seats.

In through the automatic sliding door I walked and found a reception desk staffed by a lovely grinning fella with fiery red hair set off by a blue golf shirt bearing the hotel name and a plastic name tag that read "Duncan."

"You must be the Canadian Rock Stars," Duncan said in a dialect that I can only describe as near indecipherable and awesome at the same time. His pronunciation was tricky to understand, as was the speed at which Duncan and many of the other locals in Northern Scotland spoke. However, I would soon learn that the hardest part about understanding the Scots was that they used the same words that I used, but they did not mean the same things I meant. You know, "jumper" was a sweater, "birds" were girls, and so on. Add a few curse words and you could hear a sentence like:

"Ooh aye f—k like, Alan. I cannae take the piss out of your jumper when the birds so clearly fancy it, you right c—t."

But during this first meeting, Duncan was much more polite.

"Welcome, welcome indeed. From Newfoundland, I see. My uncle worked the oil rigs there. Always good to have folks in town that find our weather pleasant." Scots could be the best laughers in the world. I still love any chance to go there and be amongst such wonderful people.

He asked a few questions about Runrig and what the guys were like, and after some polite exchanges he pointed me to a set of elevators that would take me to my room. On the way to the elevator I spotted a combination breakfast/bar area. With great fondness and joy, we later discovered the bar would be open 24/7 for hotel guests. I have always envied this in European hotels, and cursed the thousands of times I have walked into a North American Hotel at eleven thirty to find the bar closed for the night.

All you needed to get a drink at the Red Roof Inn was a room key. A single brass key that looked more like a school classroom key than any new-fangled high-tech key or key card. Attached to each key was an oval-shaped piece of blue plastic bearing the name RED ROOF INN on one side, and on the other side, a simple three-digit room number. Mine was 206.

I proceeded up to the second floor in the small four-person, polished-metal elevator and strolled down a blue-carpeted hall lined with birchy-wood doors until I reached my small room. I slid the key into the door and smiled upon entering the small but spanking-new, clean-as-a-whistle room. Two steps to the right was a small but sparking bathroom, and two more steps to the right was a double bed just the right size for one person to sleep in quite comfortably or two people jammed together. It was neatly made with white sheets, and blue pillows that matched the carpet and comforter, and a headboard the same birchy wood as the door. Two more steps and you could lay your bag on a small table with metal legs and a birchy wood top. Two small chairs with the same metal legs and birchy wood as the table were pressed against a window that overlooked the small car park.

You are probably getting the picture that the room was small. I sat in one of the chairs, and my knees almost touched the bed's headboard. Yes, the room was small, but more than I needed, and I was delighted with our hotel choice, especially considering we had the better part of a month to go in a couple dozen locations. I could not wait to see what the next one looked like.

——

Twenty-four hours or so later, we pulled into the second hotel, and the bump of the curb woke me from yet another awesome van nap. I rubbed my eyes and puzzled at the sight before me.

"Did we forget something?" I asked Bob. "Why are we back at the same hotel?"

"Wake up, b'y. We've been driving for two hours."

"This is a different hotel than yesterday?" I looked behind me to see that we were indeed in another new and cool Scottish town with a character of its own. I could not wait to explore it. I looked back at the hotel.

"Yeah, pretty similar, isn't it?" Bob said.

Similar? It was identical. Like, spooky identical. Walking through the automatic sliding door and seeing the reception desk was as *Groundhog Day* an experience as I've ever had. The furniture in the lobby was not only the same style and colour as the day before, but each piece, each table and chair leg, seemed to be in exactly the same place. Was I still drunk? I wondered as I turned to the reception desk and stifled a yelp of surprise.

"You must be the Rock Stars from Canada. Do you think the Runrig guys will be by for a drink later?" The words came from a fiery red-haired fella wearing a blue golf shirt with a nearly indecipherable but awesome accent. My eyes bulged and darted to his nametag. It read "David."

He handed me a key with a plastic blue tag that read "407" and pointed us to the polished-metal elevator that took me to the blue-carpeted hallway of the fourth floor. I pushed open my room's birchy door and took two steps past the bathroom, two steps past the bed and two more steps to the table and sat in the birchy seated chair, my knees brushing against the birchy headboard.

It turned out I was not losing my mind at all. I discovered that the Red Roof Inn's mother company had bought or leased lots in a few dozen towns in the UK and set out to modernize the accommodations industry by providing consistency across the board. You'd no longer have to wonder what the B&B in Falkirk was like, or if the Mom and Pop hotel in Stirling had a car park, because the Red Roof Inns were all the same. All the locations were built and opened within months of each other a few years before, and they were very intentionally laid out, furnished and operated identically.

It became a routine for the next two or three weeks. A new and interesting town in Scotland or Northern England with the *Groundhog Day* hotel right in the middle of it. We'd wake as late as possible and eat as big a breakfast at the buffet as we could shovel into us since the next meal was not coming till 6 or 7 p.m. I learned to maximize these meals by taking a Tupperware container to breakfast. I'd eat breakfast from the British hot section of the buffet, then sneak back to the cold or continental section and jam a bunch of cold cuts, cheeses and a couple of rolls into my container. The boys mocked me for this, but not a day went by when someone did not avail themselves of my Tupperware collection around lunchtime.

We'd check out, and a Duncan or David would say thanks and not to forget to leave our keys and wonder one more time if the Runrig guys would be coming back to town soon. We'd often just nod and smile in that polite kind of Canadian way without giving much thought. Then we'd drive to the next town, through beautiful Scottish landscapes, almost all of which I missed because I'd be asleep five minutes after we hit the motorway, and I'd be awakened again by the van turning into another carbon-copy Red Roof Inn.

We'd walk through the automatic sliding door, say hello to a Duncan or David, speculate that yes indeed the Runrig guys could be here any moment, walk to the polished-metal elevator, down the blue-carpeted hall, through the birchy door and I'd two-step two-step two-step my way to the metal-legged chair.

After a week or two it was getting monotonous to say the least, though in all honesty, I spent so few waking hours in those rooms that it did not bother me too much. I'd chuck my stuff in, explore the town for an hour or two, then arrive at the venue for our 6 p.m. sound check and 7:30 show. I did not carouse and get blind drunk every night, but I caroused and had a few sips almost every night on that tour. There were some memorable nights in the Red Roof Inn hotel bars drinking, chatting and singing songs for as long as the nightshift Duncan or David had the patience to serve us.

The most memorable night came on June 9, 2001, near the end of the Scottish leg of the tour. I can tell you exactly what night it was because the focus of our excitement that day was that the hotel bar/breakfast area had a TV with an international cable sports channel. I asked Duncan if it was at all possible for us to watch the Stanley Cup playoffs later that night. He said he'd check it out, and I strolled off to explore and do the show. There was much revelry that evening as we all had the next day off, and Duncan was thrilled to see the Runrig guys come back to the hotel bar with us sometime after midnight.

"I found your ice hockey for you!" Duncan was so excited, I felt bad to admit to him that I'd totally forgotten about the game. It was to be played in Denver that evening, and with the time difference, would start in about a half an hour.

What a night. We all sat drinking and telling stories and singing songs, but the best part was Bruce and the rest of the GBS Canadians explaining the ice hockey game to the Scots. Hearing them cheer for the fights and big hits in their local brogue was nothing short of amazing.

"Aye, wee f—ker with your caged mask and your lightning-quick glove. You'll nae give us a goal tonight, will you, you stingy—"

All the while, I explained the rules to Duncan. He was so impressed with the goalie's gear and agility, he'd regularly jump up and imitate the saves.

"You nae score in the five-hole here. Me shafts are jammed tighter together than the Queen's Gates!"

All together, we watched Ray Bourque finally win a Stanley Cup with the Colorado Avalanche. We cheered when Joe Sakic handed him the Cup, and sang and laughed and eventually succumbed to the clock not far from when night turns back to day.

Somewhat bleary-eyed I walked, not without a stumble, to the polished-metal elevator, and the shiny door closed before me. I went to push the button but realized I had no memory of what room I had checked into earlier that day. I was just about to go to Duncan and ask the embarrassing question, when I stuck my hand in my jacket pocket and felt a plastic oval tag.

"RED ROOF INN" was all it read. "Shite." But then I remembered to turn the key over. "Ha. You can't fool me."

203 was the key, and with the confidence that only comes with a night of drinking Scottish beer and whisky, I pressed the 2 button and made my way to my room. After all, I had the whole thing down to a science by now and could practically do it in my sleep. Which, in truth, was not far away. I slid the key into the lock and pushed the door with the swagger of a man who'd danced this dance dozens of times.

I nearly broke my nose on the birchy door when it did not open. I tried again, losing confidence and growing puzzled. Again and again I turned the key, but it would not budge in the lock. Hmm. Must be broken, I supposed. I turned and rode the elevator back down to the now all but empty lobby. Duncan looked surprised to see me coming.

"Sorry, man. My key is not working."

"Oh dear, so sorry. What room number is it?"

I tossed the 203 key and he caught it in his left hand, windmilling it round in the air like I'd shown him Patrick Roy doing earlier in the game. He grabbed another 203 key and fake slapshot it my way, and I made a similar Roy-ean wind-mill and got back in the elevator before the doors closed.

As the elevator doors opened on the second floor, I felt the heavy weight of the evening press upon me and practically sleepwalked down the hall to my room. I slid the key in the slot, carefully this time, as I was too tired to walk back to the lobby a second time if the door failed to open again.

Right as rain, the birchy door opened and I slipped the key back in my jacket pocket. I two-stepped in the dark past the bathroom and bed towards the familiar birchy chair. I was directing my bum towards the seat just as a rustling caught my attention enough to rouse my closing eyes.

My sight adjusted to the dim light coming through the car park window as my bum continued its slow but sure decline onto the seat. The next four to five seconds felt like an hour, as my life and a few other things passed before me.

My eyes shot to the bed as my bum continued its descent. On the far side, a figure lay on the bed, and as it turned, a long lock of blond hair fell onto the pillow. A beautiful Scottish girl was in my bed? I looked to the table next to me and saw two bags, but not one of them mine. My bum was now millimetres from the target, which meant my knees were now millimetres from the face of the second person in the bed. A Giant. A Scottish Giant. He was big—Braveheart big—the smallish bed barely holding his torso and his massive arms and legs spilling out over the sides. I could see one fist as big as a ham resting on the blue-carpeted floor.

I froze. I don't mean I was fairly motionless and quiet. I mean I froze. No movement—no breathing, no blinking, no heartbeat. I froze in a position so close to sitting yet just high enough from sitting that only a hair's width of light separated my knees from the Giant's nose. If they touched and woke the sleeping Giant, I was sure I would draw my last breath flying through the window and onto the roof of a car in the car park.

I glanced at the fair Maiden. To my horror, one of her eyes was opening. In her near sleep she whispered, "Love?"

Then again. "Love?"

"What?" the Giant responded. He did not open his eyes. If he had, I would not be telling this story today.

The Maiden looked at me with an unfocused, dream-state gaze.

"Love. There's someone in the room."

The Giant lifted his fist and rolled just enough to raise it to his face without bumping my knee. He rubbed his fist against a closed eye and said, "No, love. Go back to sleep."

With that, he rolled back into place and was about to let his ham-fist slip towards the floor when I saw that my knee was now directly in its path.

I shot straight up in breathless silence as his fist plummeted to the floor, narrowly missing my legs by mere inches. Standing now, I saw my chance to escape. I turned and took two steps, two steps, two steps to the door, making no effort to walk quietly and no effort to open the door silently. I hurried. I had not taken a breath in over an hour, remember. I pulled the door open and let it close behind me, but I cannot tell you if it slammed because I ran as fast as I could to the elevator and hit the Down button so hard I nearly broke it. When the elevator finally arrived, I pushed the G button, and gasped my first breath as the doors opened onto the bright lobby, now empty, except for Duncan with a bucket and a mop.

I was going to kill him. He'd obviously given my room away and then sent me into the lion's den. He had his back to me and did not see me coming. I reached into my pants pocket and yanked out the key for room 203. Holding it up in front of my face, I took a deep breath, about to yell as loud as I ever had.

The RED ROOF INN tag spun before my eyes as I drew my breath. I was just about to bawl like a man who had narrowly escaped death when the tag spun around and the three digits shone in the light.

307

What? I stopped. Duncan still did not see me. What was going on? I stuck my left hand into my jacket pocket and felt a second plastic tag. I pulled it out and three digits stared back at me.

203

Oh dear. I shook my head as I realized what I had done. I'd unknowingly left yesterday's Red Roof Inn with the 203 key in my jacket pocket, and when I arrived at today's Red Roof Inn, I got a new one for 307 and slipped it in my pants pocket.

I turned and walked back to the elevator.

"You all right, mate?" Duncan had finally seen me.

"Yeah, man, just had to get a drink of ahh . . ." I let the doors close before I trailed off.

I walked furtively down the hall of the third floor, fully expecting a Braveheart Giant to jump from the darkness and gut me.

I slid the key in 307 and two-stepped two-stepped two-stepped to the birchy chair and sat there as my knees hit the mattress. I was so relieved that I fell asleep in the chair. When the wake-up call from the lobby came, I was still sitting there. I got up, took my unopened bag and left the room without so much as taking a pee or lifting the bedsheets of that hotel room. I walked quickly though the lobby and laid two keys in front of a David, who must have relieved the Duncan from the night shift.

"Great night I hear! Are the Runrig guys still around?"

Rudely, I did not answer. I just shrugged and gave a final salute.

I ran to the van and closed the door behind me. I was drifting off to sleep as we pulled out of the driveway.

I stayed awake just long enough to see a large Scottish man and a beautiful blond lady companion complaining at the front desk.

It is undeniably night now. Jerry's tie hangs loose around his neck like a noose before it gets pulled tight by the Hangman. Which could very well be his fate if he does not get home soon. His white shirt has a small Guinness stain that seems to be spreading without him knowing or caring, or both.

He says he is taking the family around the Island this summer.

"Renting an RV and doing the whole Island. Only thing better would be to do it in a boat. How wicked would that be."

"As wicked as you think."

I say it like a movie title. And perhaps it should be.

IN THE FALL of 2018, I was invited to join the adventure tourism group Adventure Canada aboard an expedition ship with about 190 passengers as they sailed north from St. John's around the tip of the island, down the west coast, along the south coast, and back into St. John's about ten days later. I was to be a member of the Cultural Resource team, which meant I would be called upon to sing and entertain, as well as read from my books, but also to be a member of the crew, which meant I'd be up at 5:45 washing rubber boots and separating small, medium and large life jackets. Believe it or not, I was extremely excited for both types of duties.

I met the main crew for breakfast and started lugging the guests' luggage onto the ship. They seemed surprised to see me so eager to do the grunt work, but it was all a part of the experience as far as I was concerned. To temper the sight of it I joked with the others, "for Jesus sakes don't let my touring crew see me loading this gear or they'll expect me to do it every night on the road!" By suppertime, when the Captain called all aboard, I was settled in with the crew as both a singer and a worker, and I could not have been happier.

Shortly after sunset we sailed out the narrows of St. John's. This, alone, was a moment I have dreamed of experiencing for a long, long time. As you likely know, I've left St. John's on airplanes and in cars and vans for extended trips away, hundreds, if not thousands of times. But this place was settled by sailors and I have always wanted to join the history of people who left St. John's for a journey by the original route in and out of town, waving to people on the shore as the light of the city disappeared over the retreating horizon.

As the dusk drifted into darkness that October day, I waved and shouted to my wife and son as they came to see me off from the cliffs of Signal Hill. I couldn't wait to experience the same thing in reverse for the homecoming in a few days' time.

The following dawn found the ship anchored (I confess, I typed "parked" twice and deleted it . . . so much for the myth of my seaworthiness) just off Bonavista. I'm happy to report this is one of the outport towns of Newfoundland that seems to have survived the cod moratorium as it has enjoyed a booming resurgence in recent years. I had a few days there in August and was delighted to see the fish plant busy with boats coming and going, and the downtown's main street bustling with locals and tourists hurrying in and out of the many shops and businesses.

I would come to learn that the patrons and crew of this ship are transported ashore in Zodiacs (the inflatable or "blowy-uppy" small boats as I called them to the bemusement of the real sailors). The host team go ashore first and set up a receiving area for the guests and organize any buses or entrance requirements to local museums or trails or whatever the day wants done. On this morning I stepped into a Zodiac just after dawn as the first morning light lit the historic wooden buildings and colourful fishing boats along the wharf and basin.

There was not so much as a breath of wind and the water was as calm as a clock. Sitting on the pontoon of the Zodiac was like sitting on a comfy couch as we floated over a mirror of the harbour. It was nothing short of magical and I figured this one Zodiac ride was reason enough to come on this trip.

I loaded a bus with forty-five or fifty guests and was one of a few of the host team leading a group to Elliston, a few kilometres down the road. Elliston is known as a Root Cellar capital; some say of Newfoundland, some say of the world. Root cellars are shining examples of how we used to do things way better than we do now. These subterranean pantries were easily dug and maintained with a simple door or two, some rock walls and a turf-covered roof. In the winter climate like the one we enjoy here in Newfoundland, you could harvest root vegetables in the fall and they would last without spoiling for the entire winter. For the scientifically challenged, like myself, the simple explanation is that the temperature and humidity inside the cellar are ideal for root vegetable storage no matter what the humidity and temperature outside. Just keep the doors closed and the food deep in the cellar, safe from outside temperature swings and rodents, and you can eat your own homegrown produce all winter long. They use no electricity. They provide local vegetables to a winter climate without putting a single potato on a truck, ship, train or plane. No carrots trucked from California. No potatoes shipped from Chile.

It is tough to look at a root cellar and not think, "Why did we ever stop doing that?"

Elliston is also known for beautifully restored historical buildings and a puffin colony that is as accessible as a Tim Hortons drive-through.

And then there is the spectacular Sealers Museum and monument. Sealing was a necessity of life on this coast and it is almost inconceivable that any year-round sustainable human inhabitation could have happened here without the hunting of seals, sea birds and caribou, or anything else they could find in the winter. Sealing was laborious and dangerous work, and men and boys risked their lives daily to feed their families and to earn some extremely rare cash money. There has been more than one tragedy on the ice as weather and ice conditions and a combination of all led to the loss of so many Newfoundlanders and Labradoreans. The museum and monument in Elliston are both spectacular.

After a spin around Bonavista and a trip to the breath-taking Dungeon Park, it was back to the ship on the Zodiac couch.

Morning number two found us park—I mean docked—at Little Bay Islands, a town that was once the northeast hub of the Newfoundland cod fishery, the Labrador fishery, as well as the sealing industry. In its day, LBI had two massive fish plants: one for fresh and frozen cod products and a second plant for salted cod. It also had a large area of the town dedicated to the processing of seals. Two members of our host team hail from this town, which is all but fully resettled now. Tony Oxford and Gerry Strong had us all enthralled walking us though the hills and around the harbour and tickles, explaining how this once boomtown worked when they were kids. They spoke of constant activity and adventure working on the wharves and in boats and in the hills and on the frozen ice in the winter. Tales of due notes and sands from Africa and many more completely unsuspected stories had me curious and crying and laughing and loving every second of our visit. As we left I could not help but lament the fact that this town, like so many on the coast of Newfoundland, lives by a calendar whose days are numbered. You might not have many more chances to visit Little Bay Islands. So get on it straight away.

We anchored just off St. Anthony (insistently pronounced "Snatney" locally) on morning number three and after another beautiful Zodiac experience, I took what I am embarrassed to confess were my first real steps on the

Northern Peninsula of Newfoundland. St. Anthony is one of those places that proves you should see every harbour town from the water first. In all my years of longing to come here and asking people to describe it to me, I never once heard anyone say it is a spectacularly beautiful harbour and town. We drove around a bit later in the day and, indeed, entering St. Anthony by road is nowhere near as wonderful as by sea. It's just not the same thing at all.

Other than the harbour itself, St. Anthony is the home of the Sir Wilfred Grenfell Museum and House. I don't have time or space here to fully explain the impact Dr. Grenfell had on this part of Newfoundland and Labrador as he tirelessly brought medical care and medicine to remote coastal towns for decades.

As cool as the St. Anthony visit was, I had my eyes set on seeing L'Anse aux Meadows in person for the first time.

How I loved to tell the story of the discovery of this Norse site and was so delighted to hear the local experts confirm that it was true. The story goes that a husband-and-wife team from Norway had hunted though ancient writings and sagas and suspected that the language in them referred to some North American landing site that would pre-date Columbus by hundreds of years. The fact that this could disprove a long-accepted fact about Europeans first landing in the New World drove them to all ends of Europe and around the world in the hunt for the truth and any ruins to demonstrate that the Norse were indeed in North America. After years of searching and a lifetime of academic pursuit, they arrived in L'Anse aux Meadows and approached a local gent who introduced himself as George. George welcomed them and asked what brought them to this area. They felt like it might take a while to explain their unusual treasure hunt, so they just simplified it and explained they were looking for ruins.

"Oh yes. The ruins are just over here, see. We used to play in them when we were kids."

A few archaeological digs and a few key artifacts later and the Norse site at L'Anse aux Meadows would become one of the most significant finds in archaeological history. It proved not only that Columbus was well behind the Norse, but that the Norse completed the journey of human inhabitation of the circle of the globe when they met with the Indigenous peoples in the area.

Finally witnessing all this in person was a dream come true for this fella who had talked about it for so many years while working at the provincial museum. The site does not disappoint. Wicked visitors' centre and trails through the original dig as well as amazing recreations of the settlement. Highly recommended.

But there was yet one more special treat in store for me this day. One that perhaps takes a little explaining. I am a Canadian but was born on an island off the coast of the country that was not part of that country when my parents were born. Also, I was born on the very east coast of that island, and all of the rest of Canada is far to the west of us. So, feeling a connection to Canada as a first-generation

Canadian was difficult, as my parents and grandparents knew little about it. Likewise, feeling a physical connection to Canada was almost impossible because I certainly had never seen any of it. Not from my island, or more specifically from my part of the island.

But here on this day on the northernmost tip of our island, I could do something I had never done before in my life. I could stand on Newfoundland and see the mainland of Canada. Might sound simplistic to some, but this was a bit of a moment for me. I've left this island and crossed this country at least twenty times, but could never see one from the other. I pointed across the water as I spoke to my colleague Steve, "See that land in the distance behind me? That is the same land as Vancouver. Wild. Amazing. Well, to me anyway."

The next day we crossed the straits and visited another highlight of my many tours at the museum. Red Bay, Labrador, is the site of a Basque whaling station that again speaks volumes about early European settlement in North America.

A long overnight sail brought us into Woody Point and Gros Morne National Park.

I've been lucky to spend many days in this wondrous place over the years at writers' festivals and concerts, and just as many days climbing hills and hiking among geological landmarks. It was great to lead a group into the Tablelands, as it was one of the only hikes in the park I had not yet done.

With a week of wonderful behind me, I'd just watched the ship turn the corner and for the first time since we set sail, we were headed east, and in the home stretch. I was longing for a day with my family in my own house on dry land, but there were a few days of adventure left to find. And find them we would on the south coast.

Our first stop was really our only day in the uninhabited wilderness of Newfoundland. We sailed into La Poile Bay, past the settlement of La Poile, to a massive beach and cove. The idea was to give everyone a chance to see the untouched land for a day, and what a day it was. It must have been near 20° Celsius as we pushed the Zodiacs up the sandy beach and started on a near ten-kilometre hike up a hill without a real beaten path.

Over the next few hours, we scrambled and climbed and lifted and slid our way across some of the most remote parts of the Newfoundland coastline. It was as special a day as I've ever had hiking anywhere. Steve, the real guide for the day, put it best when he turned to us all and said, "Remember, you could very well be the first person to ever stand in the spot that you are standing right now." I don't know about you, but that has not happened to me very many times. It was a victory day, to say the least.

I woke early the next day because we were headed into Francois (pronounced "Fran-sway" by most locals). I'd seen old film footage from a TV documentary taken from the bow of a ship headed into the fjord that winds its way into Francois. It is jaw-dropping, and it has been a mission of mine for most of my adult life to see this sight with my own eyes.

Francois is nestled a kilometre or so inside a snaking fjord that should have been a setting in *The Lord of the Rings*. The fjord itself looks almost impassible. It is so narrow at points, and the towering grey and black bone-rock hills that lean over you as you make your way through it are imposing, to say the least. I kept expecting a team of archers to appear on the edge and ward us off with arrows darkening the sky. It is incredible. Slowly but surely the ship turned to reveal the town itself, dwarfed by sheer rockfaces on three sides. With hardly a tree to be seen, it was tough not to wonder how any year-round inhabitation ever happened here. I immediately wondered what February must be like with snowdrifts bailing down over the hills filling this little car-less, road-less town.

I suspect this, like many other remote outports, started as a fishing camp in the summer months and eventually people decided they could make it through the winter and gave it a go. I can't imagine what hardships those early set-tlers endured during the hungry months of February and March. And unlike Elliston described above, there was not a root cellar to be seen as the entire town sat on rock and rock alone. I mean, there is not a cup full of soil that I could see till you made it out of town on the trail up the hill. It makes Petty Harbour look like the Napa Valley.

Then, as the smoke from a few chimneys wafted up to the skies and a fishing boat or two zipped by full of scallops, it was easy to see how this fishing station made a wonderful home for people for so long. Francois is just breathtaking from every angle.

Have you ever been in a town with no cars? No roads for cars? I have been on a few resettled islands in Newfoundland, and one in Fiji, but I mean an active, still on the go, settled town in 2018 with no roads or cars? Anywhere in the world? I really don't think I had been till my first steps in Francois. What a feeling of stepping back in time.

A living museum to the strength and determination of the folks who settled on a rock in the middle of the ocean. Every step in and out of the town is on a groomed handmade path of either wood or concrete. I was instantly charmed by their efforts and drive and would take this trip once a month for the rest of my life just to spend a few hours in Francois. I loved it. And not just because we had a wicked dance up in the town hall or because someone has taken over one of the old fishing stages and turned it into a bring-your-own whiskey bar.

——

The night before made the morning after a tough rise, and I was not fully awake till I was in the Zodiac as dawn crept over the gunwale. I had no idea what Bay d'Espoir looked like and was amazed by the wide-open river and how I felt like I was on a completely different planet from the day before. We were just a hundred kilometres or so from Francois, but this waterway was not lined with steep Mordor-like hills. Rather, this river was flanked by high, colourful trees that grew right to the water. So much lush landscape bursting with reds and greens and oranges. It looked like we could jump out anywhere and start a vibrant new outpost in a matter of weeks.

Conne River boasts a very impressive reserve, and Chief Misel Joe is one of the most remarkable people I've ever met. He and his team have done an incredible job making this a vibrant and energetic place. Most notably the school has to be one of the best in the province, and the students from there are equally exceptional. Chatting with them, I could not help but be delighted with their worldly, contemporary maturity mixed with their keen respect for the ways of their elders and the past.

I was stoked to be asked to join the drum circle. A real highlight for a wannabe percussionist like myself.

Our last day before we sailed home was our one and only trip to another country.

You probably think I've gone cracked. How could we sail to the US or Europe in one day and make it to St. John's in another? But therein lies the oddity of Saint-Pierre-et-Miquelon, France. Yes. France.

To make a long story short, after a few wars and treaties and such, France opted to keep control of these two islands just off the coast of the Burin Peninsula of Newfoundland. And keep control of them they have. Saint-Pierre, again, is within eyesight of what has been Canada for nearing a century. You could be forgiven for assuming that this tiny town of a few thousand must be somewhat decoratively like France but in fact is very North American. No one would blame you for thinking they surely must drive North American cars, and speak mostly English, or keep store and restaurant hours more like Halifax than Marseilles.

But they don't. Not a single little bit.

I often describe Saint-Pierre as follows: It is France. Just a few streets of France, but France nonetheless. It is not like France, but actually *is* France.

You'd think they would fish the same way as fishermen just a few kilometres away in Burin, Newfoundland. They don't. They don't have the same kind of boats or tie them up the same way.

Their lighthouses are different.

Their shops are different, their meals are different. And yes, even their graves are different.

Saint-Pierre, France, is not just like France. It *is* France. In every way that I could see, hear and taste.

Our last night aboard the ship was jovial, to say the least. Like every night, the meals were great and a few drinks in the bar brought out some laughs and eventually a few songs. I think most were surprised to see me head to bed well before the final party started to roll. I was on a bit of a mission, you see. I knew that in just a few hours we would be poised outside the narrows of St. John's. I had a date with my wife and son to complete the circle and was not about to miss the return.

I lay restless in my bunk and did not sleep much at all. I reflected quickly on some certainties I'd gained over the past ten days. Some I expected. Some I did not.

I did not expect to be so in awe of the landscape of our island. I thought I knew it. I had no idea. I can only imagine the vastness of the Labrador Coast, which I hope to see soon. I thought I understood the significant role Newfoundland and Labrador has played in the history of the globe in the last thousand years or so. I really didn't, in any full and complete way. I still have a ton to learn. I figured I could speak to a rural way of life having grown up in Petty Harbour in the heyday of the inshore cod fishery. But my days in Little Bay Island and Francois proved me a novice at rural life.

I also concluded that I live in a very special place. One with a complicated and deep relationship to the land and sea far greater than I would have imagined. The people of Newfoundland and Labrador have become part of Newfoundland and Labrador. We are in it and of it in a way that is unique to here. We walk on it and it feels us. We sail off it and it carries us home. Or doesn't. We sing of it and it hears us. We eat it and it eats us. We are part of each other, and I love that we are.

I rose at dawn just as we passed Petty Harbour, my childhood home. As first light hit Cape Spear, I got some cell service and texted my family. They were waiting and made their way to the same place they'd been ten days ago. The red sun lit the morning sky off the stern, but this sailor took no warning from it.

I made my way to the bow and at 7 a.m. we made for the lights of St. John's Harbour.

I could hear him before I could see him. So could all the others on the deck as Cabot Tower loomed over us. He was almost as excited to see me as I was to see him.

I gathered about fifty passengers and on cue we all shouted hello to him. He was chuffed.

A wife and a son waving you into St. John's in all its morning glory. I am the luckiest person I have ever heard of.

The ship's horn sounded and the passengers and crew shouted and celebrated. There were hugs and kisses and thank yous and farewells, but I could only hear one single word.

Home.

"Oh my God, I almost died laughing." Rhonda responds to a story like so many of us do. We exaggerate the humour of it all to make a point, right? It was a funny story and we laughed a lot. Right? But we didn't almost die from laughing. It's just a turn of phrase.

Till it isn't.

The POLISH highlander

"I AM GONNA smother."

I gasped for breath but could not stop shaking long enough to take one. As I poked at my left eye sopped in tears, I just managed to utter, "I think my contact lens fell out." I blinked my vision clear enough to see that my two bandmates were faring no better and were also in grave danger of suffocation.

The back of the small Euro passenger van was winding its way from the Polish winter wonderland of Zakopane, in the mountains in the south, back to the cultural capital of Kraków.

Two hours ago, we were being wined and dined in a centuries-old resort town that must have served as the model for all the Aspens and Banffs in the world. The worn cobblestone streets, the steep A-frame cottages with snow collecting in the rooflines and smoke floating in straight columns through the windless night to a sky with more stars than darkness made for a perfect walk-in snow globe.

It was enough to make a young fella from Petty Harbour feel like he was the luckiest person on the planet.

One hour ago, we were sitting up straight awaiting arrest or a firing squad or whatever else we could imagine might be in store for us in a prison in former Czechoslovakia as two very confused Polish fellas stood outside in front of the van, spinning an atlas like a ship's steering wheel.

Our guide and translator, Marcus, stuck his head in the van and said in his thick accent: "I'm sorry, he is asking if you have your passports."

I was worried. "We don't as we didn't think we'd need them. Why?"

"No problem, no problem. But we may have took a wrong turn a few kilometres back and we are now in Slovakia." Marcus turned and walked back to argue with the two Polish fellas. Deers in the headlights. As they were arguing in Polish we couldn't understand a word, but when one of them spun around and held his hands behind his back while the other mimed putting handcuffs on him, we kind of got the drift.

It was enough to make a young fella from Petty Harbour feel like the unluckiest person on the planet.

We had been in Poland for about a week, having secured an invite to the Shanties, the famed folk festival in Kraków. Marcus was a native of Poland who lived in St. John's and in the fall of 1995, he came to Sean, Bob, Darrell and me with an idea to put GBS forward for next year's event. A week or so later when we found we'd been invited, Marcus immediately volunteered as our guide and translator for the trip. He, our sound tech and us four bandmates would make up the travelling party.

——

In the dead of winter we boarded a plane for an overnight flight to Heathrow and arrived in the English dawn. We puttered around LHR for the bulk of the morning and boarded a LOT Airlines plane in the afternoon bound for Warsaw.

Walking onto that plane was like entering a living exhibition at a well-staffed and generously funded museum. Last step on the gangway at Heathrow, it was 1996. First step on the LOT plane, it was 1956. The galley area looked like it was from a Second World War Soviet submarine, with its bulky grey knobs and handles with letters and numbers that made no sense to me. It was my first real-life encounter with an alphabet that was different from my own. The indecipherable writing on the food trolleys was particularly frustrating, and the hinges looked like they were for a sub-sea locker. A quick look to the left revealed a cockpit from a film set in 1944. Grey and green faded paint on panels with finger-worn areas around the control knobs would have stood out if it were not for the myriad of analog clocks and speedometers and VU-type meters.

"Not a digital readout for miles . . ." I must have it said

aloud, as there came a reply. The voice—almost a whisper, from an arm's length away—was deep but feminine and had an accent that stirs me to this day. "Don't worry. This plane will get you there safely. Welcome aboard." She stood about five inches above me. And the lady next to her was every bit as tall.

If the galley and cockpit were old and worn, the flight attendants were anything but. The two women who stood before me were, well, perfect. I had never met a supermodel before and suddenly I was meeting two.

"H-h-hello." My voice cracked like a teenage boy serving at a drive-through window asking if you'd like fries with your order. Smooth.

I lifted my boarding card what felt like high above my head so she could see it. I felt like an ancient species getting a lucky glance at how the finished product will look centuries from now.

A Hobbit in front of an Avatar.

"You are seated towards the back of the plane in Row 33. Find your seat and we'll be happy to make your flight enjoyable. *Dziekuje.*"

I recognized her last word as a Polish thank you, as Marcus had coached me over a big British breakfast just an hour before.

"Jen qui yuh," I said with about as much confidence as a Hobbit could muster under the circumstances. As I spoke, I reached into my jean jacket and pulled out a pocket-sized Polish-English dictionary I'd purchased a week or so before.

"*Ooooh!*" Both ladies smiled a wide smile and one grabbed my arm at the curve of the elbow. Her hand felt like silk over hardwood. "We *love* to hear people speaking Polish. Please keep it up. We will help you learn more words if you like. I am Anna, I'll be in the back with you."

"*Dziekuje,*" I said—my Polish much improved all of a sudden—and chirped up like a Petty Harbour dog who'd just been patted on the head.

The plane was arranged with a standard three seats on each side, but it seemed more cramped and stuffed than any other I'd been on as I took my seat on the aisle in Row 33 and watched as the plane loaded. I kept the dictionary out along with a notebook and began scribing phonetic spellings of words in *Polski* that I figured I might want to know. I made sure I held it up like an eager elementary school kid might do for his teacher when Anna walked by to do her final checks.

"*Bardo dobre.*" She laid her hand on my shoulder as she passed.

Marcus was grinning a wide grin across the aisle. "Do you know what that means?" he asked.

"No, but I will by the next time she passes!" I dove into the dictionary as the plane rolled down the runway and took off for Warsaw.

My eager study to impress Anna was broken by a smell I could not quite identify. I looked up and quickly clocked a trickle of smoke creeping along the ceiling above my head around the seat light and air vent. I was about to shout for help when Marcus spoke,

"Here we go. You won't see this anywhere in North America." As he pointed around our seating area, dozens and dozens of matches struck and lighters clicked and Zippos snapped.

I was so enthralled with learning how to say *"poprosję piwo"* that I'd forgot I'd agreed to sit with the others in the smoking section.

For many of you, smoking on an airplane will sound about as safe as licking a high-voltage cable. Likewise, the notion of lighting up in a closed metal tube with hundreds of others in very close proximity will sound as pleasant as sleeping in an ash tray.

Both your assumptions are correct.

In less than a minute, the entire ceiling of the airplane was obscured by cigarette smoke. And not any smoke I'd smelled before. Not in my kitchen with Mom and her friends, not on the wharf in Petty Harbour when the fishermen gathered after the boats were cleaned, and not even in the tight station wagon we toured the country in, with me the only one of six who did not smoke.

This smoke smelled, well, Eastern European. After a few deep inhales and a coughing fit I remembered I actually had smelled something similar once before when Russian sailors tied up a boat in St John's Harbour. Mom and me had travelled to town on a bus that day and were heading to

Bowrings department store when we walked past a pod of them gathered around a payphone.

"My God, they must be smoking the oil drums," Mom said as she covered her mouth and nose with one hand, removing it only to sneak her cigarette in the corner of her mouth.

Back in Row 33, the acrid odour made my eyes water. You could taste the air. And it did not taste good. I was about to stand up and try to get out of it—because nothing, and I mean nothing, I figured, could keep me in this seat—when . . .

"*Witaj*. How is your Polish study coming? Can you say some words to me, please?" I never changed my mind so quickly in my life as Anna bent at the knees before me. Her stylish hat was off now, revealing a tidy bun of blond hair that made her silver-blue eyes feel closer.

"What words do you want to know? I can help you." She leaned over my lap now to see what I'd scribbled.

"Excuse me," I said, which confused her so much she seemed about to jump up, so I explained quickly: "I want to learn to say 'Excuse me,' so I can make up for how clumsy I can be and let people know that I likely don't know what I'm doing or where I'm going."

Anna smiled. "Well, that's very nice for a famous musician." Over her shoulder, I could see Marcus giving a thumbs up behind her. "Your manager Marcus tells me you are a famous musician in Canada."

I would have corrected her about Marcus's job title, but I was too busy blushing. "Me? Us? No, not really. We plays a few places, but we're not that famous or anything."

Anna smiled broader now. "I see. Famous and modest too. You'll do well in Poland." She slipped back to stand up but stopped just before she did and looked me in the eye.

"*Prƶepraszam.*" I stared at her and prepared my marriage proposal. She repeated the word phonetically. "Se-praszam . . . *Excuse me* in Poland. Keep practising." And with that she disappeared in a cloud of cigarette smoke.

The rest of the flight went by quickly as I learned about a dozen words, including the Polish for *hello, thank you, please, love song, sorry* and *goodnight.* I had no idea how well these few words would serve me over the next week to ten days. In fact, they served me so well that I make it a practice every time I go to a land with a new language to always learn to say *excuse me, please, thank you* and *sorry* before I learn anything else. How Canadian is that?

We landed in Warsaw, where we were greeted by a much smaller van than we expected and spent the next two hours roaming around the city trying to find a way to send our equipment on a train. By the time we left to drive to Kraków, it was already early evening and we had not slept in a couple of days. Darkness set in very quickly as we made our way for the Polish countryside and all we could hear from the front of the van was a language we did not understand. Meanwhile, Marcus was sound asleep and no help to us.

"The trees look like Gorky Park," I said aloud, but I'm not sure anyone heard me. The misty, smoky darkness wrapped around the van as we drove headlong into the night.

We arrived in Kraków at about two thirty in the morning—pretty much forty-eight hours since I had been in bed. We walked under a hotel sign that I could have sworn read "Damn Thirsty," but I assumed that was just the sleep deprivation. You can imagine my surprise when I woke the next morning and walked out to see that I had almost got it right.

The Dom Turystyczny in the central part of historic and impossibly beautiful Kraków was to be our home for the next week. And what a week it was. A pair of guides around our age were assigned to us to help negotiate our way through the festival, but they also took it upon themselves to make sure we had the time of our lives while in town. They took us to all the night spots after the gigs but would not let us sleep in and miss the cool cultural stuff either.

We'd be out till 4 a.m. and they'd have us up at eight to tour the castle, or visit the salt mines, or eat in a famous Jewish restaurant. We never stopped and we were the hit of the festival by every estimation. Most of the other acts were extremely folky or groups of older men in funny throwback costumes singing in unison. We, on the other hand, were in our mid-twenties, dressed like Pearl Jam and treated every show like it was in Madison Square Garden.

I am not bragging when I say they loved us. At the closing concert, they gave out seven awards. We took five of them. And on the last night they wanted to wine and dine us one more time and invited us to the festival's closing dinner up in the incredible historic resort town of Zakopane.

———

The night in Zakopane was amazing. The drive over the Slovakian border was terrifying. To ease the tension, we sang a few songs with the gang in the van. Me and a couple of bandmates towards the back with our assigned guides, the two Polish fellas in the driver and passenger seat, respectively, with Marcus right in the middle, translating from the Polish front to the English rear.

I'm not sure what started the "Highlander" song. It may have been that we needed to lighten the mood after the border incident and one of us Newfoundlanders sang one of the funnier Newfoundland songs, like "Johnny McEldoo" about a fella on an eating binge, but safe to say something prompted the Polish fellas to respond in kind.

Now, dear reader, a note on what is to follow. I will attempt to describe what is one of the most ridiculous situations I've ever participated in. In doing so, I have to describe what I heard from the front seat, which of course was in Polish. To represent what was beyond my powers of comprehension, I'm going to use some of the few Polish words I know and fill out the rest with the word *Polskie*. This is meant in no way to be disrespectful of the beautiful Polish people or their beautiful language.

So when Marcus leaned forward between the driver and passenger seats, I heard: *"Polskie, Polskie, Dziękuję, Dobre, Polskie."* And then Marcus turned back to us with a grin so wide his teeth lit the van. He giggled like a schoolkid as he spoke.

"Hehee ha . . . They would like to sing for you a Polish song."

"Awesome!" We all figured this was a great addition to the night and a great way to pass the next hour before we made it back to the Damn Thirsty.

"Heheee. Okay, okay." Marcus turned back to the front.

The two Polish fellas started singing. It was as much of a chant as a song. They sped up as they went through what I assumed was a verse that led to a final line that ushered in a chorus.

"*Polskie, Polskie, Dziękuję, Dobre, Polskie* . . . *Polskie-polskiepolskie* . . . HAHAHAHAHAH!"

We grinned in the back as clearly something in this song made them crack up. They almost put the van off the road, they laughed so hard. Marcus was trying to stop laughing and was gathering himself to tell us something.

"Oh my God, he is going to try to translate for you," said Sylvia, one of our guides, face-palming.

"Okay, okay. Hehee." Marcus was getting himself together as he turned around to face us in the back. The two guys in the front went silent with excitement. Like two kids waiting for their dad to sit on a whoopee cushion. One spun around fully in the passenger seat and the other started looking way more in the rear-view than through the windshield.

"Okay, okay. Hehee," Marcus repeated, his childhood Polish accent thickening with every sentence. "There is, you see, a Highlander, who has been in the mountains. And he has heard a bell ringing for the dinner. Hehee . . . he is hungry, so he runs down the hill? Do you understand so far?"

"Yes, I think we got it so far." I was desperate to hear what was so funny.

"Ha!" The van swerved as the Polish driver slapped the steering wheel. He could not wait for Marcus to continue.

"Okay, okay. Yes, he is running downhill, you see? But it has been raining and he slips and . . . Hehee . . . HIS SWORD COMES OUT AND CUTS HIS DEEEEK!"

"HAHAHAAHAHAH *POLSKIEPOLSKIE* HAHAH!" The sight of the Polish contingent absolutely losing it was a funny sight to behold. We laughed heartily ourselves—at the ridiculousness of our current circumstance mostly, and the fact that the silly fellas were so hell bent on telling us a dick joke.

The Polish fellas took our laughter as encouragement to continue, which they did with a glee that a child might have under the tree at Christmas. The sped up the chant more now and hit an even greater laugh crescendo at the end.

"Polskie, Polskie, Dziękuję, Dobre, Polskie . . . Polskie-polskiepolskie . . . HAHAHAHAHAH!"

Sylvia face-palmed again. The rest of us could not help but roar with laughter at the sheer joy being had by Marcus and the Polish fellas in the front. It took Marcus a minute or more to collect himself and wipe the tears from his eyes. His nose was still running when he turned back to us.

"There is, you see, a Highlander, who has been in the mountains in the winter. And he has heard a bell ringing for the dinner. Heehee . . . he is hungry, so he runs down the hill? Do you understand so far?"

We laughed as we nodded.

"Okay, okay. Yes, he is running downhill, you see? But it has been snowing and he slips and . . . Heehee . . . HE HAS FALLEN IN ICY WATER AND NOW HIS DEEEK IS FROSSEN!"

"HAHAHAHAHAHAH." The entire van was laughing now. I saw Passenger Fella reach to hold the van wheel while Driver Fella wiped tears from his glasses.

The fact that Marcus was all but repeating the same story verbatim was cracking us up but lost on him and the Polish fellas, who assumed our laugher to be about the story itself. This started a laughing cycle. A perfect storm. A tornado had begun to spin and there was no stopping it now. Everyone's laughter fuelling everyone else's. And not for the assumed reasons, which made the whole thing even funnier.

It continued and escalated for the next thirty minutes. Each verse taking longer to tell in Polish and translate as the laughter was now approaching debilitating. Marcus had lost almost all sense of his second language and was almost completely unilingual by the last few verses.

"Piwo prosze dziękuję."

"Aha, whooo. Yez. Yez.

"Okay, okay. You see, the Highlander wass runnink down dee hill and he has found himself slipping towards an, ahh, *przepraszam*." He turned around to confer in Polish.

"Piwo prosze dziękuję. HA. HA HA!"

He turned to continue: "Yez, yez, he iss runnink and towards the butcher shop. He is so hungry for meat, that he is runnink too fast and slips through the store and goes right into the back of the big cold area where there are . . . *przepraszam.*" Marcus confers once more. "Where there are HOOKS. CAN YOU GUESS WHAT HE HAS HOOKED ON DEE HOOKS THIS TIME?!"

I could barely utter a word, I was so out of breath, but someone had to try to get to the end of this before we all choked or were driven off the cliffs between Zakopane and Kraków. I managed: "His dick?"

"YAAASSZZZ! He's DEEEK!" shouted driver and passenger and Marcus in unison now. The Polish fellas' conversion to using the English DEEEK almost killed me.

"I am gonna smother." I really thought I might.

Luckily the lights of Kraków came into view and finger-pointing and directions took over the conversation and I could give my guts a break. When we reached the hotel we were barely able to hug our goodbyes as my sides were so sore.

I collapsed in the bunk and was woken early by a call to meet in the lobby for the airport and the long journey home.

I was tender from cheek to waist, like someone had body-checked me for an hour. I walked to the bathroom to brush my teeth and put in my contact lenses, but my eyes stung as I tried. I turned to the mirror to notice I had broken a blood vessel in my eye from laughing.

With my hair in a mess, body tender and listed off to one side and my glasses on over one teary eye and one bloody one, I made my way to the lobby's pay phone with my trusty international calling card in hand.

I had to call my parents before starting the long journey home, as I had not spoken to them since I left. Dad's monotone "h'lo" was a welcome familiar sound. I told him about the incredible experiences of the past week or so when he asked, "And what about last night?"

"I almost died. About six times, really. Once in Slovakia and four times in near car accidents." I was rubbing my face trying to wake up and didn't realize I may have alarmed him.

"Jesus be careful. You mother will go cracked if anything happens to you." Dad successfully deflected the concern and continued. "And what was the sixth near-death experience?"

"Laughing. I almost died laughing." I was not quite finished speaking when Dad added.

"Well, b'y. That's not a bad way to go."

I sat silently as we rode to the airport in Kraków through the most beautiful place I'd ever seen in my life. As I boarded the LOT plane to start the journey home, I looked for Anna, but I could not find her. A gentleman flight attendant looked at my boarding pass and pointed to the back of the plane with a smile.

I spoke to him, but what I said was for an entire country, for the experience of a lifetime.

"*Dziękuję.*"

I love St. John's. I used to think it a big,

unfriendly city when I was a kid growing up in

Petty Harbour. As many rural Newfoundlanders

do, I assumed it was as my grandparents warned:

a faceless and cold mass of people. But it is not

like that at all.

This pub is a St. John's pub. Like the city

itself, warm and friendly and full of curious

people eager to meet you and help you do whatever

you want to do.

Sometimes I don't even deserve the place.

I AM A SCATTERBRAIN. I am easily distracted. My hands are constantly inked with notes and times for appointments. My iPhone buzzes and chimes constantly with calendar alerts and reminders. Mel at our office and Andy on the road are charged with the most unenviable task of reminding me what I am supposed to be doing, and when I am supposed to be doing it.

My poor, suffering wife has devised many ways of attention-grabbing, reminding and corralling the two generations of Doyles who share her house. Our son and I would chase a red pen light around the floor like a cat if she flashed one. Without a list on a sheet of paper glued to our heads, she could send us to the convenience store for milk and we'd come back an hour later with a record from Fred's, an ice cream stain on our shirts from Moo Moo's and a hubcap from Kings Bridge Service Station.

Like Father. Like Son.

Our initials read ADHD.

Yes, I am a scatterbrain. I have accepted this about myself from a young age and, with the help of many patient others, I function almost like a regular person. But no plan is perfect.

For many years, two of the ten houses on our little street in St. John's were occupied by older gents. Mr. Murray and Mr. Bowering were both in their eighties and shared the near-superhuman ability to engage you in interesting banter and tidbits of history about the world, country, province, city and even the street itself. Both gents, you see, lived on this tiny street in the oldest city in North America for their entire lives.

"Mr. Bowering, Mr. Murray, how are ye?" I'd regularly greet them as they gathered on the pavement between their houses. Their response was as dependable as a well-tuned clock.

"Still alive, b'y. Still alive," one or the other would invariably say. Then we'd launch into a chat about how soldiers or goats once roamed the meadow now occupied by my house or some other fascinating historical nugget. I was charmed by their passion for the place and how much pride they took in remembering the tiniest of details from decades before.

"All together, ye gents have lived on this street for 150 years or more!" I joked to their grins during one of our usual chats in the middle of the road. The road was not much more than a path when they were kids, so they still seemed surprised to see a car rounding the corner, and even more surprised that modern convention required us to step aside and interrupt a grand yarn for something as unimportant as a fire truck.

Mr. Murray was the older of the two, and Mr. Bowering had recently had a health scare, but the pair were still quite active gents. I'd often see Mr. Murray in his small front yard tending to a few flowers and would always pause to wave and offer comment on the weather. His smile was infectious, and it was impossible not to smile back. And when Mr. Bowering was not busy recalling to you the U-boat he spotted in Petty Harbour in the 1940s or something, he would pursue his favourite pastime: driving his tiny red vintage convertible.

He had a special Tilley hat that he wore with one flap up while driving with the top down, and the engine sang a putt-putt song that purred over the mono AM radio as he rounded the corner of the street. Mr. Murray always waved a happy wave as he honked the car's clown-like horn. A one-man parade for us and us alone.

I think I can speak for everyone on our street when I say we felt very lucky to have these gents so close to us.

And so I was saddened to receive an email from a neighbour a couple of doors down the street one evening while I was touring in Winnipeg. I had barely time to read it, as I was walking onstage to do our sound check a few weeks into a month-long tour opening for Barenaked Ladies. One of the tricky things about the opening slot is you have to be ready just as the headliner finishes their sound check, usually around 5 p.m., and get your stuff onstage and checked by 5:30 so the crew can all make dinner call. So, I was in a bit of a rush when my phone buzzed in my pocket, but as it was an unusual email from home, I wanted to read it right away.

"Let's roll. We got twenty-five minutes!" One of our crew guys was pushing a drum kit on a riser with wheels.

As I was walking to my mic position with a guitar in one hand and my phone in the other, I stopped mid-stride when I read that Mr. Murray had passed away peacefully in the night. I did a silent "Cheers" to him and planned to do a more fulsome and fitting remembrance when time allowed. But just as I was about to step to the mic, my phone rang. I saw that it was my wife, so I answered right away.

"Doyle, come on, we got like twenty minutes!" I felt our audio tech whiz past me with a mic stand.

My wife, Joanne, was calling about a travel detail, and I responded in haste since I was being rushed downstage centre.

"Yeah, Monday on the 11:50 flight. I'll grab a cab as it will be late. Gotta scoot for sound check."

I was about hang up when I figured I should comment on the loss of Mr. Murray, which I assumed she would have heard about long before me. I should not have assumed so.

"We are down one good man on the street. Sad."

"What? Oh my, what happened?" she was struggling to hear me over the kick and snare drum behind me.

"Doyle, please, we got seconds here. Can we get this done?" Our sound tech was near shouting next to me now, while on the phone, Jo was desperate for specifics.

"Was it Mr. Bowering?"

A scatterbrain does not do well answering two questions at once. A scatterbrain's ear can, at best, hear and process one thing at a time. And at this time, I only clearly heard the voice of the fella standing next to me speaking into a mic being amplified by enough PA to fill the SkyDome. So, I said yes to him and went back to the conversation with my wife, who reasonably assumed the yes was in response to her question.

"Oh my, that's so sad," she said.

"Yeah, terrible to lose such a good fella. He'll be missed. I gotta scoot to sound check. Buzz you later."

I hung up the phone and launched into a quick sound check. We finished just in time for catering and ran to the trough. About thirty minutes later my phone rang and again I saw that it was my wife. When I answered, I could tell it was on a speaker phone, and all I could hear was Jo and our neighbour David panting and yelling. I was instantly worried.

"Wait, wait, what's up? I can't hear you."

They described to me the events of the previous thirty minutes on our quiet little street in St. John's.

When Jo hung up the phone with me earlier, she walked to our neighbour David, who was just getting out of his car. "Did you hear?" she said. "Mr. Bowering passed away last night."

"Oh no." David was as saddened as Jo. They spent the next ten to fifteen minutes talking about what a lovely man he was and how we all enjoyed his chats and company. But the respectful remembrances and questions about when the services might occur were interrupted by an eerily familiar sound.

Jo's and Dave's eyes widened as an approaching engine in the distance sang a putt-putt song over a mono AM radio. They looked at each other in disbelief. Could they be hearing what they thought they were hearing?

They turned to the street, and their eyes confirmed the ghost they were hearing. Mr. Bowering rounded the corner in his red convertible, his hat propped up on his head. As he passed them, he waved and blew the clown horn.

They were not certain if he had shouted, "What's up? You look like you just saw a ghost!" as he drove by. As far as they were concerned, they most definitely had.

In the coming days, memorial and funeral services were held for Mr. Murray. He was a great man, much loved by all on our street and beyond. I was on the road but sent my condolences from afar as best I could.

When I returned a week or so later, I busied myself with catching up with the to-do list of a husband, dad and homeowner who had been away for a month. As I put the early morning recycling out on the sidewalk, I clocked Mr. Bowering waving to me from his driveway. I approached him to offer my regrets about recent events.

"Mr. Bowering, how are you?" I offered my default greeting to him as we gathered on the pavement between our houses. I should have expected his response, but, as a scatterbrain, I forgot to remember my gaffe from a week or so ago. He calmly said,

"Still alive, b'y. Still alive," and I almost died myself.

There's a point in every decent Friday night when all good sense is cast aside and the foolish rule the reasonable for a few hours. I live for these hours, and as Jerry is yelling into his cellphone trying to order a pizza to his house to buy him more pub time, I know fully well that we are into these hours I cherish.

I never like to see anyone overdo their celebrating. The trick is to celebrate as much as possible without having your current celebration hinder the possibility of future celebrations.

Sounds easy enough . . .

The BOY & The DRINK

I STARTED MY love-love relationship with having a sociable drink many years ago in my little fishing town. As young
men, you see, we often worked side by side with fishermen
on the wharf, helping them load and unload fish, clean boats
and tables, sharpen knives and generally act like grown-up
fishermen.

When the fishermen were done toiling for the day,
they would often have a cold beer to reward themselves for
their hard work and to quench their thirst on hot summer
days. And if you were a hard enough worker as a kid and
demonstrated enough maturity, the fisherman would look
the other way if you snuck a cold bottle of beer yourself. In
hindsight, I am sure this was done to show the younger

gang that if they acted like grown-ups, they would be treated like grown-ups.

The Golden Rule seemed to be:

Do your work, behave yourself, and you'll be treated like a grown-up. Any laziness or acting like a fool and you'll never be allowed around again.

I was one of those fellas who showed early on that he could handle his share of the work. And so me and a sociable drink became quickly acquainted, getting along quite famously after long days on the wharf, and in my teen years at gatherings on Friday or Saturday nights when my brother or sister hung around with the older teenagers.

I enjoyed how it cooled me off on hot days and warmed me up on cold nights. But what I really enjoyed was how it made me feel: taller and funnier, more willing to sing songs for the teens and to show off for the older girls. And I noticed that when these older gang had a tipple, they tended to be easier to entertain and let me stick around. Of course, there were the few who inevitably overdid it and got sick or in rackets. But in general, I found that a drink or two made everyone the happier and the times more jovial.

Imbibing became a good friend to me and remained so as I grew up. I knew from my days on the wharf that the privileges of an adult beverage would be taken away if I let my work and behaviour slip. So I vowed I'd never let it interfere with school or work, or get me into fights or any of the other negative things that it sadly brings to others.

We had a good relationship, the drink and me. I loved the drink, and, I think it is fair to say, the drink loved me.

But no relationship is perfect. I'll relate one hiccup, so to speak, in fairy-tale fashion for my shame and your amusement.

——

The Boy and The Drink had been getting along wonderfully together on their Island in the Middle of the Ocean. One day, The Boy was called to a Faraway Land, known to him as the Mother Country, to sings songs with his mates. The Boy and his mates were excited to sing in this place, and so they took an overnight journey in the sky from their Island to this Faraway Land—the United Kingdom.

Upon arrival, they decided to call upon their old friend, The Drink, who threw open the doors immediately. Now I should say, The Drink has many nicknames and personas. Sometimes it likes to go by a silly name, like Bubbly. And Bubbly is a perfect and honest name for this side of its personality, as one often feels quite bubbly with him. Other times, The Drink wants to be called Captain Morgan or Old Sam. These are dark and dirty gents, so use accordingly. Different as they are, these are honest and upfront faces of The Drink. No deception involved. They are as advertised.

On this day in the Kingdom, however, The Drink insisted on being known as Scrumpy Jack. On the surface, Scrumpy was sweet and sugary with hints of candy apple. Surely

Scrumpy Jack was as harmless as this honeyed nectar suggested—the perfect host for The Boy and his mates in this Faraway Land. What could go wrong with such a light and crisp thirst-quencher? But as this day wore on and they danced into the wee hours, The Boy began to sense something sneaky about Scrumpy.

Was Scrumpy Jack really the sweet and jolly fella he claimed to be? Or was he secretly casting a wicked web in which to entangle the innocent Boy? Was Scrumpy Jack hiding something sinister?

Regardless, they danced. And they danced. Through the morning, afternoon and night, The Boy danced with Scrumpy Jack till sleep took hold and they slid into bed together back at the Inn, far too close to dawn.

On most occasions, The Boy and The Drink fell asleep together happily. Overnight, The Drink would drift away unnoticed, and in the morning, all that was left was a hazy afterglow and fond memories of yet another wonderful night together.

But on this morning, sleep would not provide enough cover for The Drink to slip away. Just an hour or two after The Boy closed his eyes, a knock bolted him from slumber as the Inn Keeper opened the door. The Keeper had been knocking for quite a while and was angry that The Boy had slept through his alarms. He was not alone. The Inn Keeper escorted into the room a Fair and Lovely Lady who had an appointment with The Boy and his friends to bring their songs to the Kingdom. The Boy would later learn that this

Lady was called a Publicist, and she was to usher him and his singing mates to a grand castle known as The BBC.

The Boy was not feeling well at all. He wanted to explain that The Drink was still with him and that he did not wish his friend to accompany him to The BBC Castle. Moreover, he wanted to go back to sleep. But he recalled the Golden Rule from the wharf.

Do your work, behave yourself, and you'll be treated like a grown-up. Any laziness or acting like a fool and you'll never be allowed around again.

The Boy had agreed weeks before to visit The Castle, and his singing mate, Fiddle Player Fella, was waiting downstairs. He knew that refusing to go was unthinkable. Though he really wished his friend The Drink away, he would just have to tag along.

And so the four of them made the journey to The Castle—The Lady, Fiddle Player Fella and The Boy with The Drink still clinging to him. They sat awkwardly facing each other as they rode in a funny-looking cab that drove on the wrong side of the street, winding past a snaky river and large clock towers, past knights and princesses and beggars and buses that appeared to spout a second bus on top. The Boy wished The Drink away as hard as he had ever wished for anything in his life. But The Drink held on stubbornly.

When they entered The BBC Castle, The Boy nipped into a private washing chamber and tried his best to urge The

Drink away. He moaned and heaved and pushed from the depths of his belly, but The Drink's hold was just too strong.

The four continued their journey into the Bowels of the Castle, where people spoke and sang in Radio Rooms, and Wizards magically cast this talk and music through millions of homes and cars around the Kingdom. Just before The Boy and Fiddle Player Fella were to enter the Radio Room, The Boy found another private washing chamber and made one more attempt to persuade The Drink to take his leave. He begged and pleaded for them to part ways, but The Drink would not stir. And so The Lady, Fiddle Player Fella, The Boy and The Drink entered the Radio Room, where they were met by a kind and gentle BBC Wizard. He had a welcoming smile and a soothing voice, the kind that made you want to relax and chat with him over a warm cup of tea.

They began talking about the music from the singing mates' Island in the Middle of the Ocean. The conversation was going quite well, and everyone seemed content. But then something changed. Quickly. Just as the conversation turned towards The Boy's songs and writing, The Drink wished to make his departure. He offered little warning of this sudden and most definite switch in attitude. A few moments before, he was going nowhere. Now, he was most insistent about taking his leave.

"Not now," The Boy instructed The Drink. "You should have left earlier if you wanted out. There is no place for you to go. You'll just have to wait till we get to a safe place for you to exit."

But The Drink had his mind made up, and there was no reasoning with him when he was in this kind of mood.

The kind and gentle Wizard asked The Boy about a personal and tender song he'd penned for a beautiful maiden.

"Yes, my writing has always been influenced by my little fishing town. Hasn't it, Fiddle Player Fella?" The Boy said.

Fiddle Player Fella, who would not know the answer to the question but was wise to the ways of The Boy and The Drink and their dance the night before, jumped in and spoke eloquently about The Boy's writing while The Boy made a last-ditch effort to convince The Drink to stay put. But it was too late for that. The Boy felt his mouth slowly crack open like a prison gate pressed with the strength of a thousand convicts clamouring to escape, and The Boy could hold the tide no more. In desperation, The Boy grabbed a wastepaper bin that lay by the kind and gentle Wizard's feet. The Drink, seeing its opening, torpedoed into the bin, leaving The Boy grasping a now very messy wastepaper bin in shame.

The Boy felt terrible and embarrassed and wanted to run out the door, forget about his work and go back to the Inn and rest without the company of The Drink. But he remembered the Golden Rule, and quick as a fox, he jumped back into the conversation.

"That's right, Fiddle Player Fella. I do love to write romantic and lyrical things about loves lost. I suppose it is the parting of a much loved one that brings us the most pain and need for healing. Let us play the recording of this story for all the people in the Kingdom."

While the recording played, The Boy ran back to the private washing chamber to clean the messy wastepaper bin. He returned to the Radio Room as the recording ended, calmly sitting back in his chair next to the confused and shaken Wizard.

"Lovely, isn't it?"

The Wizard was flustered.

"The song, I mean," clarified The Boy. "Lovely, isn't it?"

"Ah yes. Yes, of course," the Wizard uttered, sinking back to his old kind and gentle self.

And on the conversation went.

The Kingdom that morning heard an insightful chat and some lovely tunes, blissfully unaware of the tug of war that The Boy waged and lost with The Drink within The BBC Castle walls. And when the work for the day was finally complete, The Boy saw the rest of his singing mates at the Inn and, sure enough, The Drink was there, sitting brazenly among them. But The Boy was very angry at The Drink and wanted nothing to do with him and shouted a warning to all:

"Scrumpy Jack is a Liar!"

My sisters have joined Bernie and me so all the Doyle siblings are present. I am lucky to have an older sister and a younger one. Makes me feel like I get a broader understanding of the opposite sex, especially considering one of my sisters is organized and sensible and the other is, well, like me.

We are not a full pint in when our family chat goes to our favourite collective topic, our parents.

I think we all agree that our Mom is organized and sensible and our Dad is, well, like me. Or I suppose, more truthfully, I am like him.

The eye rolling about our Mom and Dad is nothing but a way to show how much we love them, of course. We Doyle kids are lucky to have such amazing parents, who always made us feel as though we had so much when, in retrospect, we had so little.

The pints and laughs are good, so I won't say it aloud and shine a sincere light on a happy night of embellishment. But I whisper it to my whiskey so it does not go unsaid.

"If I do one thing in my life, I will strive to be as good a parent to my son as Mom and Dad have been to the four of us. ."

Parenting

"DAD, YOU ARE famous, right?"

My son, Henry, was around six years old when he began to realize that my job was different than his pals' dads'. I was chuffed that my only offspring might think highly of me, so I was quick to respond with some thinly veiled modesty.

"Yes, yes, I'm famous in some places, I suppose. Places where people like my music mostly."

I could see him in my rear-view mirror as we drove across Water Street in St. John's. His head was turned to the side, the way he does when trying to figure something out.

"Are you as famous as Ed Sheeran?"

I would have to backpedal.

"Ah, no, no. I'm not as famous as Ed Sheeran."

I could see him turn his head even more and furrow his brow. Something clearly did not add up for him, and I worried that my brief special dad status was in jeopardy. When he spoke again, I knew I should be.

"But aren't you older than Ed Sheeran?"

"Ah, erhm, ah yes, I am." I was about to try distracting him with a Popsicle, but I was too late.

"So, you've been singing for way longer than Ed Sheeran. Why aren't you as famous as him?"

"Oh hey, look—Dairy Queen!"

———

The transition to becoming a dad is tricky for any man, but especially if you are like me and the circumstances of your child's young life are radically different from the circumstances of your own early life. I was born the third of four kids into a very modest house in a tiny fishing town to an incredible mom and dad who were not very well off financially. We barely had indoor plumbing. My parents spent every waking hour trying to make enough money to feed us and pay bills, and they accomplished this by kicking the kids out of the house each morning and exclaiming, "Don't come back till dinnertime."

Because I lived in a village that looked after all the kids, it was a safe and fun do-it-yourself childhood surrounded by my brother and sisters and cousins. When we were out of the house, we were never far from the watchful eye of one of the moms around our tiny harbour.

On the other hand, my son was born the one and only child of a large posh house in the historic part of the biggest city in the province to a mom and dad who are quite well off financially. We, his parents, spent every waking hour doting on him and combing all the books and internet articles we could read to help us manage the minutiae of his wants and needs. If we put him out on the street in the morning and said, "Don't come back till dinner," two things would happen within a half hour. One, Social Services would show up on our doorstep to take our clearly abused child away from us while, two, the provincial media would storm our street as rumour quickly spread that the "Ordinary Day" singer fella kicked his kid out into the street.

Because he is an only child, he hasn't in-house peers to show him the ropes, and we currently live in a time when it is not just a suggestion that parents schedule their kids' lives but a sworn responsibility to schedule and administer their kids' lives and to assess that schedule on a daily if not hourly basis.

The generation gap could not be bigger than between the day my dad became a dad and the day I became one. Neither is better or worse. I'm convinced of that. Henry's young life and my young life were blessed with advantages—very different advantages, but advantages just the same. But it is safe to suggest that very few of the practical issues I have with parenting were bridges my parents had to cross with me and that I could reflect upon to help navigate my way through the parental fog.

There are a few things about being a somewhat well-known musician that augment this situation. I don't mean the constant travelling, as that is also the situation for anyone working offshore or in the oil patch. Those parents are on the three-weeks-on/two-weeks-off schedule. And I don't even mean the constant conflict of the responsibilities between one's family and one's fans. Like when Henry was born on July 4, 2006, a few weeks ahead of schedule, and GBS was to play the Molson Amphitheatre on July 6. I was so grateful to be there when he was born, and so gutted to have to leave him and his mom before they got home from the hospital. But that's not what I'm talking about when I say that being a parent as a well-known person brings with it very interesting circumstances.

When Henry was about eighteen months old, Jo and I took him to the supermarket, and as he was in a Lightning McQueen phase, we chose the big, fiery red car–wrapped supermarket cart. He loved getting strapped in behind the plastic steering wheel in the toddler safe seat and driving around as we zoomed through the racecourse he imagined in the fresh fruit and vegetable section. It was all going well till a particular odour started to make its way across the broccoli and cauliflower that announced in no uncertain terms that Henry needed a change of pants in that way that toddlers often do at the very worst possible times.

"You get the groceries and I'll change him in the van." Jo was halfway out the door with him before I could volunteer to do the same, so I carried on and turned the corner to the bread aisle.

As I continued with the grocery duties, walking through the bread aisle, a lady smiled a long smile at me. But it wasn't a smile I'd seen before, the one where someone recognizes someone they saw on TV or in concert or whatever. This lady was more amused than excited. It was curious to watch her stifle a giggle as she passed me.

A few steps later, two young fellas in their twenties obviously recognized me and made no effort to stifle their laugh.

"Ha! Look at Buddy! You're cracked, b'y," they said, nearly bent over and slapping their knees.

I found this confusing. I regularly shopped at this supermarket and was used to chatting with people who recognized me, but something was very off today. I scanned the events of the past few days and wondered if I had been in the news or on the internet doing something funny. As I was considering the possibility that my friend Mark Critch had done a particularly good impression of me on *This Hour Has 22 Minutes*, a mom giggled at me while her toddler son pointed as they passed.

I rounded the corner and came face to face with my friend Nick, who immediately burst out laughing.

"Nick, why the frig is everyone laughing at me today? Is my fly down or what?"

Nick laughed even more when he realized I did not see what was so humorous. I was grateful that he leaned in to whisper discreetly instead of broadcasting the explanation.

"Jesus, Alan, b'y. You're a forty-year-old walking around the supermarket."

"Yes, but I does that all the time. What's the big deal?" I leaned in to Nick.

"Alan . . . you are pushing a Lightning McQueen kid cart. With no kid in it. You are lucky people knows you and have not phoned the cops to come get the pedophile at the grocery store."

———

You'd think my own house would be a safe space. Not at all.

"Oh wow, are you a builder?" Henry had just returned from preschool and ran through the kitchen into our pantry, having heard hammering and seen carpentry tools lying around. He was into a bit of a Bob the Builder phase and becoming more interested in saws and hammers than Thomas the Tank Engines.

"Yes, I'm building cabinets for your pantry." Paddy is an expert cabinet maker and has the added appeal of looking like a cowboy movie star with his long white hair and enormous moustache. I was in the next room but could clearly hear him speaking with Henry from high up a ladder.

"What about your dad? I bet he builds stuff too."

And when Henry responded, I almost spit out my coffee.

"My dad? A builder? No, no. He's just a Rock Star."

My friends in this corner have mostly been my friends for decades. My family, forever. Perry since I was three, and almost everyone else since I moved to St. John's over thirty years ago. I am still Bernie's brother to many of them. I am Tommy's young fella to many more. And I wouldn't have it any other way.

St. John's is like a small town when it comes to fame. Everyone is glad you got it, but don't you dare act on it around here or you'll be put in your place pretty quick.

When a fan asks for a photo at the Duke and seems genuinely glad to see the famous Newfoundlander fella on home ice, it is both encouraging, as I'm always delighted to meet folks who want to meet me, and terrifying, as I know I am getting the gears when I get back to the table.

Being a famous Newfoundland fella in Newfoundland is not like being a famous fella anywhere else . . .

You Should Say When You're Buddy

I NEEDED TO rent a van to move some furniture from St. John's to our family cabin in rural Newfoundland.

I called several local branches of a national rental company, and they all explained they were out of vans as it was a busy long weekend. One final branch agent who introduced himself as Mark offered a glimmer of hope, albeit a distant possibility.

"B'y, there's a couple coming back around noon, but there's a lineup as long as your arm to get one of them. Give me your name and I'll do my best for you."

I was eager to get in the line and quickly said, "Cool. Thanks so much. My name is Alan Doyle."

There was a brief pause on the line, and Mark seemed either confused or alarmed and I could not tell which.

I hung up the phone and got a cab up to the rental agency by the airport with equal parts hope and doubt. I sent the cab away when he dropped me in the parking lot, so I suppose hope was leading.

I entered the strip mall store entrance and was met with Mark and two others behind the counters, straining their necks and waiting in anticipation. As I entered, Mark and one of the others high-fived and shouted, "I told you it was him! I told you it was Buddy!" (which locally means "That fella in particular) while the other rolled his eyes and hung his head in defeat. As he raised his head again, he reached into his pocket and he handed each of his friends a five-dollar bill.

"Yes!" Mark was exuberant as he waved me to the counter. "I knew it was you. Dougie here wouldn't believe it."

Mark continued as I approached the desk, not completely sure what was happening. "Jesus Christ. You're in luck, Alan Doyle." He called me by my full name, which made me oddly uncomfortable. "There's a van just pulled in and you can have it, for sure. Wasn't sure it was you on the phone, but glad to help you out."

Then he finished with a statement that makes my head spin to this day. "You should say when you're Buddy."

———

When I was very young, I idolized my uncles, who played in the town's band in Petty Harbour. I was not the only one who held them and their bandmates in high regard. It was like they always got a longer leash than others, allowed to stay at the parties as late as they wanted. As a ten-year-old, as I was learning to play guitar and sing, I became clever about when I would offer to sing songs for my parents' friends when they were at the house. I knew that if I waited till later in evening to start, I could put off my bedtime by a few hours by strategically breaking out the John Denver songs for my aunts.

"Ten thirty, go to bed now, Alan honey," Mom would say, and I'd quickly grab Dad's guitar and start into "Country Road." The second I was finished that one, I'd blast into "Thank God I'm a Country Boy."

"Jesus, Jean, let him stay up for another bit," my aunts would insist, and Mom was put on the spot. If I was cute enough about it, I could make it till well after midnight. The big home run was to save "Leaving on a Jet Plane" till about 1 a.m.

I was aware at a very young age that people might like you just a little bit more if you sang to them. I came to learn that it was really a reciprocal love affair. I wanted to sing for them as badly or more as they wanted me to sing for them. So the "fame" part of being in a band started as and remains more a mutual appreciation than anything else.

I was beyond grateful when Great Big Sea became a band that more and more people wanted to see. I was used to the popularity and longer leash that the Doyles had in Petty Harbour with people who knew my uncles personally, but I was not at all used to people who did not know us personally wanting to contact us. So, the only way I knew to handle that kind of attention was to treat it personally.

Our first piece of fan mail was from a girl and her friend in the Topsail Road area of St. John's. They had written to the address printed on our first CD, which looked like a business address but was really one of the guys' parents' house. They asked for a signed photo. I got the lads to sign one and was going to pop it in the mail, but as my only experience with fame had been in person, it felt weird to mail it. That felt a bit too pretentious for me. So, I drove to their house and hand-delivered it along with two T-shirts. They seemed thrilled. Their parents seemed legit concerned.

As we started touring around Canada, we were blessed by the diaspora of expat Newfoundlanders who not only came to see us in droves but also dragged all their new friends from the local area to our shows. It made for an odd fame in retrospect. The rooms were always half filled with people who had never seen anything like the four of us with our shanties and accordions, while the other half was filled with people who felt like they knew us intimately.

The diaspora was really responsible for paving our way across the country, and we were incredibly grateful to them. Every night there was a pre-show party and an after-show party in Calgary or Red Deer or Edmonton or Fort McMurray. They wanted us to go to every one of them. And we felt like we should. By the end of our first week in

Alberta, I was nearly dead from socializing. It was impossible to go to a pre-show and post-show party and still play six to seven shows a week.

Some folks were extremely disappointed. I cannot tell you how often I have said,

"Wow. Thank you so much for the pre-show supper invite. That is extremely kind of you. But I cannot eat a full jiggs dinner before our concert. But, again, thank you very much . . . What's that? After the show? Oh, after the show I have to go to sleep because tonight is show two of seven in a row and I have to make sure I don't lose my voice."

The disappointed looks of "Ah man, you are after getting too big for your boots" haunt me to this day.

I began to suspect that being a famous fella from Newfoundland is not like being a famous fella from anywhere else. Especially if you sing any kind of traditional music, you might find yourself in circumstances most rock stars would not.

We had a very brief period when we were in our mid-twenties when girls our age would come to us and say, "I love your band."

It was flattering to feel like a rock star for a moment, but I never paid much attention to that kind of attention as I was too eager to keep the band rolling. I figured that kind of attention would go on as long as the band did.

I was wrong.

Very quickly, by our late twenties even, girls of that age were walking up to me and saying, "My mom loves your band," along with the occasional, "I'm here with my aunt Brenda. She *loves* you guys."

I figured it would never get worse than that, and indeed the "My Mom Loves Your Band" phase went on for about a decade. But all good things come to an end, and outside the House of Blues in Chicago it happened. I should have seen it coming, but vanity is a cruel master.

She was a beautiful twenty-something and I was a well-worn thirty-something. She approached the tour bus as I was being escorted to it by a football-player-sized security guard.

"Can I tell you something?" she asked.

I stopped. I needed an ego boost. And this attractive lady telling me her mom or aunt likes my singing would carry me through another day or two for sure.

"Hey, I'm Alan," my customary greeting as I'm never 100 percent sure people actually know who I might be.

"Of course you're Alan, silly. I just saw your show." She was the perfect match of eager and cool. I stood up like a peacock.

Here it comes, I figured. Her aunt is a big fan, totally taking it for granted. Then she spoke.

"My nan loves your band."

"Excuse me?" I wasn't sure I'd heard it correctly.

She gestured to a vehicle parked just behind the bus. "My nan loves your band. I brought her to the show. She's in my car behind your bus and wants to meet you. She can't stand much longer. Would you mind coming back to say hi to her?"

"Ah . . . yeah . . . ah, sure." As I spoke, the football-player-sized security guard. grabbed my arm.

"Careful, man, this sounds like a trick."

Before I could consider his caution, I heard Nan shout out the window: "Hello, my love." She sounded like my mom and I instantly recognized a Marystown, Newfoundland, accent. "You had me bawlin' tonight singing 'Wave Over Wave' and 'Lukey's Boat.'"

I spent the next twenty minutes leaning in the passenger window of a compact car, talking with a lady in her early seventies from the Burin Peninsula who had married a US Navy officer she'd met on a base in Argentia, Newfoundland in the late 1950s. We figured she'd graduated school in Marystown a year or two ahead of my mom and knew all my aunts and uncles.

Our chat was finally broken when the young lady broke up the reminiscences.

"All right, Nan. Enough flirting with the band. I got to get you home."

A few through-the-window hugs later, they were off and I walked on the bus with the full knowledge that the "my mom loves your band" phase was over and the "my nan loves your band" phase had begun.

I figured having Nans love your band made me feel a bit old but in the end was a pretty good result. And surely nothing could ever trump this phase.

I was wrong.

In the spring of 2015, in the middle of the Come Out with Me Tour, a gal in her mid-twenties approached me at a pub after a gig. I stood up straight and was ready for a nice Nan compliment, but when she spoke I was almost knocked on my arse. Apparently, there are phases beyond "my nan loves your band." I sat back on the bar stool and shook my head when she exclaimed, "You were my mom's first concert."

Jerry's tie is on the floor. His hands are waving more than his lips are moving. The Guinness spot on his shirt has spread to the size of a hockey puck. He is begging any and all of us to go home with him to continue the party, but mostly to keep him from getting bawled out for being late.

"Lotsa grub home, b'ys. Come on back—we'll get a midnight barbecue on the go."

None of us fall for it. Jerry's gonna have to face the music solo.

A song from the opposite corner breaks Jerry's pleading. Someone is singing along with the stereo, which is playing "Grey Foggy Day," an unlikely song of celebration, as it has been adopted to champion our poor weather.

An unlikely song can save you, though. This much I know.

I DROPPED IT

"HEY, MAN, can you play the lute?"

Russell often opens his telephone conversations as if you had been discussing something thirty seconds ago, when in fact you may not have spoken with each other in months. Russell had been a pal of mine for four or five years by the end of 2008, when he asked about my medieval instrument capabilities. I had grown accustomed to his peculiarities—as he had to mine—so I did not even pause to comment on what an odd question he had just posed.

"Yeah, man. I can play bouzoukis and mandocellos and lutes and all that stuff. What do you need?"

I assumed Russell wanted some tracks for a new song we'd written or some background music for a film he was doing, or something along those lines. I did not expect him to say: "Ridley Scott and I are doing a Robin Hood film and there's a role you'd be great for in the Merry Men. Allan A'Dayle is the musician, and he needs to be an Irish-sounding bloke who can play the lute and write and sing songs on the spot. Could you come to LA with your lute next Wednesday and do a table read for the part?"

An hour later, I left the concert venue in Ottawa where I had been sound checking and took a cab to the Ottawa Folklore Centre to buy a thirteen-string lute.

I was going to Hollywood.

———

Late in 2003, I had heard a rumour that Russell Crowe was a fan of GBS and my songwriting. A fan from California told me she'd just seen his band, 30 Odd Foot of Grunts, and they'd covered a song of mine called "How Did We Get from Saying I Love You." I had no way of confirming this but most certainly wanted to believe it because, well, holy frig—how cool would that be if the world-famous Gladiator is singing a song I wrote about a chance meeting with an ex-girlfriend on the bridge in Petty Harbour? I figured I would never get a chance to just stroll up to an Oscar winner and say, "Oh hey, man, I'm Alan. Heard you dig my tunes," so I more or less put it to rest on my lifelong wish list.

Then in June 2004, I was stoked to be sitting with NHL stars at their awards show in a posh theatre in Toronto. I had been asked to hand out the Rookie of the Year award at the last minute, and every inch of my body believed the organizers did this because fate would want a Newfound-lander like me to hand fellow Newfoundlander and nominee Michael Ryder the trophy. (When I looked at the card at the podium and it said Andrew Raycroft was the winner, I almost said the wrong name, but that's another story.)

When my award presenting was done, I took my seat and was surprised and delighted to hear Ron MacLean introduce the next presenter as "Academy Award winner Russell Crowe."

I can't even remember what trophy he gave out as I was too focused on the single task of creating an opportunity to accidentally bump into Russell backstage and introduce myself as the one who wrote that song he likes. I still owe Edmonton Oilers hero Ryan Smyth an apology for stepping on his foot as I awkwardly pushed my way through the aisle to get backstage. When I got to the hallway where the pre-senters and winners were gathered together chatting, I posi-tioned myself by the main exit and tried my best to look like I was there by complete coincidence.

I saw Russell making his way through the hall towards me and the nearby exit. Practically everyone wanted to speak with him, and he exchanged pleasantries with each of them as he came closer and closer. I was worried that he'd be sick of chatting by the time he got to me.

I had rehearsed a very unrehearsed-sounding "Oh hey, man, you're Russell, right? Yeah, congrats on all that Oscar-winning stuff and being an internationally famous movie star and all that, but more importantly, I heard a rumour that you might like one of my songs." I was preparing to deliver my lines when something unexpected happened. Russell Crowe turned towards me and spoke first.

"Hey, man, you're Alan Doyle, good to meet you."

I think I just stood there with my mouth open or something and Russell was forced to speak again. "Love your tunes, man. You guys are playing the Molson Amphitheatre in a couple of weeks, right? Yeah, a bunch of us are coming. See you there."

Mouth still open, I just nodded. He was just about to make his exit when that part of your brain that screams "SAY SOMETHING!" at times like these kicked in and I came out with some words and then joined those words to some more words and then, well, I'd be lying if I told you I can recall now what exactly I said. But I'm betting it was something like this, in the thickest 1985 Petty Harbour accent I default to when nervous:

"Oh hey, b'y Russell . . . We are playing in a couple of weeks . . . certainly happy to put tickets aside for you, but you probably got tickets or people to get tickets for you, whatever . . . certainly happy to have you and we'll play that song you likes, or at least I heard you might like from some missus in San Francisco or whatever . . . and sure we'll probably have beers after the show backstage and you could come and have one of them or even two or whatever if you wants and meet the fellas 'cause they loves movies too."

I then realized I hadn't responded to his original statement and quickly added, "Oh and yeah, I'm Alan."

"Cool, man," he said. "See you then." And with that, Russell Crowe and the largest rugby-player-looking security guard I'd ever seen turned and exited onto the Toronto street.

I figured that was that, and I'd likely never hear from him again. But as I walked offstage before the encore at the Molson Amphitheatre show in Toronto a few weeks later, a pal tugged my arm and whispered, "You've got Russell Crowe here, my dear."

After the show, Russell and his gang—including the big rugby-player-looking fella who I would come to learn was Australian Rugby League legend Mark "Spudd" Carroll—hung with all hands backstage. It was such an incredible feeling of validation that this international star had taken a night out of his life to see us and that he enjoyed what we did as much as we enjoyed what he did. You could feel the excitement and satisfaction up and down the halls. If that had been all there was to it, I would still be smiling to this day about the experience.

But there would be so much more to it. Just as the night was closing, Russell offered: "I'm in Toronto for the next couple of months, with weekends off. Are you ever passing through on a Sunday? Perhaps we could write a song together?"

I was quick to accept the invite, saying, "Man, I pass through Toronto every Sunday in the summer as we usually play festivals Fridays and Saturdays. I could pop in for sure. That would be amazing."

By the end of the summer, I had spent a dozen nights or more hanging in Russell's camp as he shot the film *Cinderella Man*, and we had written and recorded a couple of songs. By January, I was in Australia producing a full CD for him and a newly assembled band called The Ordinary Fear of God. From 2005 to 2008, we had written songs for his projects, my projects and third-party acts like The Ennis Sisters.

So when Russell asked me if I played the lute, I assumed it would be for some song or CD or soundtrack, and my head spun for days after the invite to a table read for *Robin Hood*. I can't tell you all the people who sat in on the table read, but I can tell you I was so nervous that a few minutes before we started I called my brother, Bernie. He said, "Jesus, Alan, you are sat at a table with the Gladiator and Batman. I suppose you are nervous."

As I sat with a guitar propped against one thigh and a lute propped against the other, a tableful of seasoned actors—and me—read through the screenplay. I said my lines as Russell advised—"in your own natural accent, as it is very Irish-sounding to almost anyone"—and I sang the bits that needed singing and did not break a string or have a heart attack. I got the part.

At the end of March 2009, Great Big Sea played the last song at the Juno Awards in Vancouver. I left the stage and went directly to the airport and flew overnight to London, touching down in England before the dawn. At arrivals, I met a gent named Tom who held a sign with my name on it.

After a few pleasantries, Tom confessed that he had googled me, which made me feel famous. Then he confessed he'd done so "because you are one of the only people in the principal cast that I'd never heard of," which made me feel not famous enough. I needed to change the topic.

"Tom, are we headed to the rental house they got for me in Richmond?"

"No, mate." He reached behind his head with a yellow legal-sized envelope. "Straight to set, they said. I imagine that's your scenes for the day in there. Ah, who am I kidding. You seem like a gent who likes an honest man. Don't rat me out, but I read it all when I was waiting for you this morning. You got two scenes. Lotta arrows to shoot and a fight scene but only one line of dialogue. You'll be grand."

Right to set? Lines? Fight scenes? All of this sounded fine and dandy when we were training and practising a few weeks back at Russell's farm, but today, the reality that it was upon me made me queasy.

For the next hour I sat in the back seat as Tom explained in great detail how Arsenal were by far the best football team in the Premiership. But all I could do was read and reread the four words in my one line in the script that I was to deliver in a scene today:

1 Robin
2 They
3 Are
4 French

I had never considered how many ways a four-word
sentence could be said. Should my character be surprised?

"Robin, they are FRENCH?!"

Or did Allan A'Dayle know this all along and need to be
sure Robin knew too?

"ROBIN, they are French."

Or did our characters have a bet and Allan was proud to
announce that he'd predicted it properly?

"Robin, they ARE French."

By the time we turned off the motorway just south of
Farnham, I was mesmerized. I walked onto the set of *Robin
Hood* in Bourne Woods in the same clothes I wore on national
TV in Vancouver less than twelve hours before. I am sure
I still had the confetti from the show in my hair.

The scale of it all was overwhelming. Horses and produc-
tion trucks stretched for a kilometre. Trailers for cast and
staff were gathered like a town twice the size of Petty Harbour. A perky and professional lady with wellies on her feet
and a headset and mic on her head greeted me with a smile.

"Hello, Alan Doyle. Welcome to your first day. Everyone is excited to meet you."

The next hour and a half saw me ushered into and out of
about five departments, one right after the other, with an
efficiency I'd never seen before. Administration had me sign
documents and take house keys and a cast cellphone.

"Keep that with you at all times, okay?" Jaysus, was I
becoming a secret agent or something?

A lady named Janty ushered me into a wardrobe trailer with fitting rooms and asked me to try on all the stuff I'd need in the film. Soldier's uniform, chain mail and a few other bits all fit me, to all of our relief, and I had not taken the boots off when I was ushered into a hair and makeup trailer.

"Jesus, you are bloody PERFECT! YOU LOOK LIKE A MEDIEVAL HOBBIT!" I was not sure how to react to this man's excitement as he pulled my beard and lifted some of my long hair into a ponytail. "Just make him dirty and we are good to go!"

I was led to a trailer that had two doors, one on either side. One had a sign that read "Allan A'Dayle" and the other read "Will Scarlett." As soon as I rounded the corner, the Will Scarlett door swung open.

"ALN DILE!" Scott Grimes loves to pronounce my name the way it would have been said in Petty Harbour when I was a kid. And to tell the truth, I love when he does that too. There's more talent packed into Scott's shorter-than-average, red-haired, freckled frame than anyone could possibly imagine. He is an incredibly versatile actor who's done everything from playing a teen on *Who's the Boss?* in the 1980s, to *Party of Five* in the 1990s, to *Band of Brothers* in the 2000s and over a hundred episodes of *ER* between 2003 and 2009. This is not to mention dozens and dozens of other roles on hit shows like *Dexter, Justified, Suits, Shameless* and *The Orville.* He has also been the voice of Stevie Smith and others in over three hundred episodes of *American Dad* and *Family Guy.*

Scott hugged me reassuringly as I bet he knew I would be sh—ting myself, and started talking as he walked me down the length of the trailer. He spoke till he opened my door and closed it behind me

"How was the gig in Vancouver, heard you killed it, and you are going to kill it today too, pal, it all must look a bit much, but you were made for this, I'm telling ya, get your stuff on and we'll walk through the scenes together, oh man, this is gonna be fun, buddy, this is gonna be fun."

The door closed behind me and I surveyed a fifteen-by-eight-foot room with a couch and a table with dressing room lights surrounding a mirror. A door between them led to a bathroom with a sink, a toilet and a shower. Many might think this a small place to work and live in during the day hours for four months, but you have to remember, I usually sleep on a forty-foot bus with ten other people. This trailer was like the Shangri-La as far as I was concerned.

My calm moment of satisfaction was broken by a knock on the door by a hand so big and strong that it could only belong to the mighty Little John himself. Kevin Durand swung the door open and almost ripped it off the hinges in the process, as his massive Thunder Bay frame bent and squeezed through the door.

"*Allons-y!*" Kevin's French-Canadian heritage always comes out when he is excited. He grabbed me around the waist and lifted me to the trailer ceiling as easily as you or I would lift a newspaper to our face. Kevin is a trained musical theatre actor, singer and dancer who defies all expectations constantly. Despite being six foot six and 250 pounds of muscle, he is a ballet dancer who got some of his earliest training at the Charlottetown Festival and in the musical *Guys and Dolls*. He then kick-started an incredible run as a TV and film actor that would take him to Hollywood and beyond. On the small screen, he had starring roles in *Lost* and *Vikings*, and his big-screen credits run the gamut from *Smokin' Aces* to *3:10 to Yuma*.

"Ah, Alan Doyle, how cool is this?!" Kevin was right. This was super cool and, in many ways, he was responsible for it all.

One of Kevin's earliest movie roles was in *Mystery, Alaska*, where he starred with Scott Grimes and, you guessed it, Russell Crowe. At a cast party one night, it was Kev's turn to spin some tunes. Kev spun some of his faves, which just happened to include a band from Newfoundland called Great Big Sea. When the song "How Did We Get from Saying I Love You" came on, Russell asked Kev to replay it and then wanted to know who was singing and who was the writer. Kev explained both were me, and if he had not done that, none of this would have ever happened.

Kev and Scott and I were in medieval costume as Allan A'Dayle, Little John and Will Scarlett when the same perky and professional lady in her wellies poked her head around the corner.

"Merry Men, Robin Hood is out of hair and makeup and would like to see you in his trailer."

The boys strode down the plastic walkway laid over the mud and I paused for a moment to check myself. Many of the people I'd played with on the Junos show the previous night would not be out of bed yet, and here I was about to walk in full costume onto a film set with Russell Crowe.

It was hugs all around as Robin Hood and his Merry Men met outside Russell's trailer on day one of shooting. I paused again to survey the moment. I was not visiting these fine actors on their film set. I was with them on our film set. Their collective histories and resumés washed over me and I actually felt nauseous.

Russell Friggin' Crowe, Oscar winner with a career on screen and stage for well over three decades—easily one of the top ten, if not top five most successful actors in history—joked with Scott and Kev as I stood uncharacteristically silent. The gap between their skill sets and mine was almost making me sick to my stomach.

Did I mention Scott could very well be the best vocalist I've ever met in my life? Did I mention he was on Broadway when he was ten? Did I mention he toured with Bob Hope and Michael Jackson as a feature singer? Oh, did I mention Kevin was in the friggin' *X-Men*? Did I mention Ridley Scott was the director? Did I say Cate Blanchett was arriving in a few days?

I'll stop now. I just want you to know the depth of the talent pool I had waded into before taking the one more step that would find me at the bottom of a learning curve so steep I thought I'd never see the surface and breathe again.

The first scene we shot featured Robin and the Merry Men cresting a hill to discover a band of soldiers stealing from a group they had just ambushed and killed. My job was to trail behind the others, hide behind a log with Russell and, on cue, say my line. Four words:

1 Robin
2 They
3 Are
4 French

"Action!" Max, the assistant director, was waiting for nothing to get the cameras rolling.

We crested the hill quite well. I did not trip or stumble. I made my way to the log and said . . .

Well, I didn't say anything.

I opened my mouth and nothing came out but dry, dusty air. I tried to swallow but couldn't. So I gave the talking thing another go.

Have you ever seen the teenage boy character on *The Simpsons* who usually works the drive-through at Krusty Burger? The fella whose voice lets you know he's in the midst of puberty as his voice cracks while asking, "Would you like fries with that?"

Well, that young fella's voice was cooler-sounding than mine was when I finally managed to speak on the *Robin Hood* film for the first time.

It went something like: "Raw-BUN, Day ahRR FA-wrench."

I almost face-palmed myself, I had botched it so badly, but a few seconds later the scene was over and Max yelled,

"Cut it. Back to ones, please." Which I came to learn was first positions.

I walked back in silence, and the guys did not say a word. I was convinced their silence meant they were all reconsidering my ability to do this. Back at ones, it remained silent for what felt like an eternity.

"ALAN DOYLE'S FIRST SCENE EVER!" Russell and the boys shouted. They were putting me on and hugged and congratulated me and the crew joined in. "Your film cherry is busted! Welcome to the motley crew!" someone shouted, and someone else added, "Welcome to the dark side!"

It was the exact icebreaker I needed. They'd told me, without actually saying it, that they had my back. They all did. The most learned people in the biz were going to help me through it. And they did, time and time again. Over the next few months I was given a master class in film, and I needed every bit of that on-the-job training as I found myself making every rookie mistake ever heard of, and a few that no one ever had.

The next day we had a massive fight scene where I was to run down the hill and shoot two arrows. Russell explained before we started, "Be as stealthy as you can and shoot straight like we've been practising, and whatever you do, don't stop. Just keep going. This is a big scene and you are just a small part of it. If you cock up your bit, but keep going, the cameras will capture lots of other stuff, but if you stop, you'll ruin it for everyone. So keep going, okay?"

"Got it." And I was sure I had.

I had not.

Max called action and a couple dozen actors and horses and stunt people took flight. I ran down the hill like an assassin. I grabbed my arrow perfectly, but as I went to notch it, it fell to the ground. I lifted my head, turned to Max and said with a voice that sounded not like a medieval Irish soldier but the kid from *The Simpsons* again, "I dropped it."

Max shook his head and waved me down the hill.

I figured he did not hear me.

"No, I said I dropped it!"

"Cut!" Max may have added, "For f—k's sakes," or that might have been someone else. But I definitely heard it.

Back at ones, Russell just grinned a grin that really did not need to be explained.

"Take 2. Action!" shouted Max, and off we went again down the hill perfectly. I drew the first arrow and notched it like a lethal killer, sending it into the fray below. It was an amazing feeling. We were doing it. I was doing it. I was so excited that I forgot to concentrate on the second arrow. I reached for it and it fell to the ground.

I cannot explain to you why I did what I did next. I wish I knew.

I stood up and looked back up the hill to Max and said, "I dropped it again!"

"CUTTTT. JESUS f—king Christ!" It was definitely Max speaking now.

Back at ones, Russell repeated the instruction from earlier and added, "Look around, man. All these people love you and want you to do well. But now you are keeping them from their lunch."

One look at the hungry crew, and I never dropped another arrow for the next four months.

The lads helped me tremendously as I constantly made gaffes you would not think possible. In one riding scene, the three Merry Men were to chase after Robin as we peeled out of a goodbye scene with Maid Marian. It had to be done at impressive speed, and Scott was worried his slower horse might not keep up. A lagging Will Scarlett would not be welcome for this shot.

I was encouraging him to lift the reins and lean into the gallop and all would be well. Will and John and Allan would stick together and it would be awesome.

"Action!" After a line and a kiss between the hero and heroine, we blasted down the trail behind Robin Hood. Will and John and Allan were all in stride. It was looking so cool and was definitely going to make the movie cut. And then I shouted across the frame: "Attaway, Scotty!"

"Cut!" Max waved us back. And Scott tried not to laugh as he said, "You are doing good, pal, real good. Let's just try to call each other by our character names and not our real ones."

Later, when we finished a scene where I had a line that went something like, "Let's go over to the tree and get the horses," Kevin called me over.

"You are doing good, bud. Real good. But when you say 'tree,' you don't need to point to the tree or trace the outline of a tree while saying it. They might cut in a picture of the tree and even if they don't, I'm pretty sure the folks at home know what a tree looks like."

"Got it." And I was sure I had.

I had not.

We shot the scene again and Kev called me over again.

"You are doing good, bud. Real good. But when you say 'horses,' you don't need to hold your hands in front of you and pretend you are holding the reins. They might cut in a picture of the horse and even if they don't, I'm pretty sure the folks at home know what a horse looks like."

Russell Crowe, Scott Grimes and Kevin Durand showed me more patience and kindness and guidance than any man deserves in a lifetime. I love them dearly for it.

With the help of Robin Hood and the Merry Men, I made it through the first month, and by the time the midway point of the shoot rolled around, I was becoming more comfortable, learning to focus on bringing all the talents I could to the mix. I had a history of writing sea shanties, so I wrote a few and recorded them in a makeshift studio in my tiny trailer. I wrote "Bully Boys" for a scene where Robin Hood and the Merry Men return from France to England, and the song became a feature in the film and later a big part of one of my CDs and live set.

They also wanted my character to "sing" the news—to respond in song to events in the scenes. I had experience as one half of a live comedy duo and could write funny stuff on the spot. I never thought that skill would be useful on this job, but you never know when you might be just what the doctor ordered.

A curveball came one day when a fight scene was changed at the last minute. Scott came to me nervously on set as we waited for Ridley and Russell to come from the writers' meeting.

"Hey, have you seen the changes?" I explained I had not. Scott handed me a copy of the new scene, the paper still warm from the printer. "Dude, there is a song in this scene?!"

"What?" I grabbed the sheet and glanced over it quickly. There, at the bottom of the sheet read, "All the while A'Dayle sings a song about a large-breasted woman."

"Dude, what are you gonna do?" Scott was nervous and a little put off that they would land me in this spot.

"I am gonna sing a song about a large-breasted woman," I said, hoping I looked as confident on the outside as I was terrified on the inside.

I walked in the woods and considered it all. A few moments later Russell and Ridley arrived on a four-wheeler and approached me with grins on their faces as wide as a cat who'd cornered a mouse.

"You read the new scene?" Russell was almost laughing now.

"Yes, sir." I turned to Ridley as he was giggling now too.

"Do you have a song for us?"

"Yes, sir. Would you like to hear it?" Ridley turned and waved me over to set, saying, "No, I'm sure you've got something, and we'll learn a bunch if we shoot the rehearsal."

"Action!" Max looked like he was in on the joke as well.
I sang:

Nancy, you're me darlin'
I loves you all to bits
I'll climb up to your chamber
And on your mountainous t—

Then the dialogue interrupts my bawdy song, and the scene continues.

To this day, "Large Breasted Woman" is one of the biggest earners in my song publishing catalogue.

A song has breathed new life into the place. What was once fading is now blossoming again. Jerry's found his tie, for frig sakes, and is asking for soda water to clean his shirt.

A song saves the day. Funny how often that happens.

I MISS DOWNSTAGE centre. People have kindly commented that it looks to come naturally to me. It didn't. I
learned and studied and practised and failed for many years.
I continue to learn and study and practise and fail. Well, I
was doing those things until the middle of March, when
COVID-19 did the unthinkable and shut down every single
stage on Earth simultaneously.

I miss it desperately. Standing in front of groups of
people and facilitating their good times has been an important part of my life. I miss the band and the hangs and the
crowds and the bus and the late-night gas station corn chips
and the wink across a 5 a.m. Air Canada plane to a bleary-
eyed bandmate that says "This is horrible" and "My God,
how lucky are we" at the same time.

I'm not sure who said this first, but it is true: "The only thing worse than being on the road is not being on the road."

I started on the side of the stage. If you are lucky, you will too.

Since the inception of the *American Idol* TV show and ones like it, I have worried about young singers and how some of their earliest performances are on international TV. My first two hundred performances were inside my buddy Brian's garage with a barbecue lit to fend off the February cold. We stank of chicken wings, and we stank. We could barely get through one song. Until one day we did. Then we got through two. Eventually, we could do a three-song set for a school concert and, later, half of the school dance. Then a full one.

Downstage centre is a much easier spot to handle if you have made your way there gradually over time.

My uncle Ronnie had many bands that played up and down the Southern Shore. The venues in these fishing towns were not pubs as you might imagine. These towns had clubs with large dance floors, and on Friday and Saturday nights the band had one job and one job only: keep the dance floor full and the drinks flowing to the thirsty dancers. When I was just fifteen years old I started playing in bands with him. I was way over on the side of the stage, one of a couple of guitar players. I watched and learned for most of my teenage years.

Ronnie would sit behind his drum set, survey the club and instantly decide if we should start with a fast or slow song. If people seemed to be listeners more than dancers, we'd play a few lyrics-driven ballads or easy listening songs sprinkled with a few jokes in between. But if they jumped to the dance floor on a Friday night, Ronnie would run four or five fast dance songs together without saying a word.

Watching him over a nest of knotted cables and rusty, bent cymbal stands kick-started the quest of my life.

I remain a dedicated student to it all, but here's what I've concluded so far.

Fronting a band each night is a cocktail of humility and confidence. Gratitude and swagger. Modesty and bravado. Bashfulness and balls.

The first trick is to realize this. And many don't learn it early enough, if ever. The second trick is much harder: you have to know how much of these ingredients is required each night if you're to get the cocktail right. For 99.9 percent of the gigs you'll ever do, you can't even begin to estimate it till you walk onstage.

No one gets it right all the time. The great ones get it right most often.

Watch Bono and U2 on what is arguably the greatest live concert film of all time, when their Elevation Tour rolled though Boston. The whole show is available on YouTube. This was at the height of their international fame and during a four-day sold-out run in one of the biggest sports arenas in the world. Surely this would be the place for all bravado, all the time. This would be the time to come in on a harness from the heavens in an explosion of awesomeness.

Not at all. Humbly the band took the stage with the house lights still on, and the first thing Bono—the biggest rock star in the world—does is kneel. He genuflects in humility and gratitude. The whole scene creates an otherworldly moment for the fans, yet makes it instantly human. They came to cheer for gods, but the gods weren't having it. The lights, the knee—it's loud and clear: "This is a night we'll have together. Not you here to see me. Not me here to do a recital for you. Tonight we are the lucky few to be in this place and time. Let's go." Over the next hour and forty-seven minutes, there was not a person in that room who did not feel blessed to be there.

The modesty of that moment sets the stage for the buildup to many Rock God moments to come in the show. And as the whole thing started in such an unassuming nature, these moments are augmented in a spectacular fashion. Gratitude leads to swagger for the win.

Compare that to Freddie Mercury and Queen at Live Aid. A completely different situation that required a completely different cocktail. The band had twenty-one minutes in the middle of a day-long procession of the biggest musical acts on Earth to prove that Queen was the best stadium act in history in front of seventy-two thousand screaming fans who'd spent half a day standing in the sun.

There had been expressions of gratitude and sombre reminders of the dire situation in the malnourished world. There was no time for bashfulness. This cocktail was 99.9 percent balls.

At 6:41 p.m., Freddie Mercury trotted onto the stage like a stallion at the gates waiting for the gun. He pranced to the piano and played the intro to "Bohemian Rhapsody," quite possibly the greatest stadium rock song of all time. They were taking no prisoners. If there was any doubt about Mr. Mercury's cockiness, he took one of those precious twenty-one-minute-long slots and just had the crowd echo his vocal exercises. By 7:02 p.m., it was game, set, match. Queen rules.

When I moved to St. John's to go to university, I was quickly immersed in pub culture. Small rooms with small Celtic bands or solo singers instead of four-piece rock bands was the fare. And much to my dismay, no dance floors. The bulk of my apprenticeship of keeping the dance floor full was not applicable in these situations. So I had to learn a whole new frontman skill set.

I started studying the popular musical comedy acts of the day, many of which were very adult in nature. Long before political correctness, there were several acts around Atlantic Canada who commanded the pub scene. Acts like MacLean & MacLean and Lambert & James played acoustically and sang parody songs with less than wholesome but hilarious content. Their between-song banter was even less wholesome, as they would basically abuse everyone in the room with locker room insults and jibes.

Still underage, I snuck into a bar on Water Street to see Lambert & James one night. As I entered, they made fun of my jacket to the knee-slapping merriment of the drinkers at the bar and at tables. "Look a' Buddy sneaking in the back there with his sister's coat on. Does that come in men's?!" Two bearded men wearing baseball hats had the place in the palm of their hands.

When they played and sang, they were very skilled and could fill the room with strumming and solos and harmonies. But no matter how good the music was, the patrons' attention would always drift during the songs unless they got to sing along. And they did, almost all the time. If the clubs on the Southern Shore required you to keep the dance floor filled, the job here was to continuously engage the audience with jokes or singalong songs or whatever it took to keep their attention. My first gigs in the pubs of St. John's, either on my own or in a musical comedy duo called Stagger & Home, were modelled after the pub masters I was lucky enough to see.

When Sean and Bob and Darrell were looking for a new addition to form a new band, they wanted someone who was schooled in this exact skill set. The combination of the traditional music skills the boys already had and my eagerness to engage the room quickly made GBS the most successful act in downtown St. John's in just a few months. One of our early tricks was to do Celtic pub versions of popular rock songs. Our version of Slade's "Run Runaway" became a pub hit so much that when we were eventually signed to a major label, this song was our first single and video. The same trick that worked to get people's attention in the pubs worked on the MuchMusic video station too.

It wasn't long before we graduated from pubs to theatres. I remember an early GBS gig at the Arts and Culture Centre in St. John's. It was a big deal to have a pub band play in the one-thousand-plus soft-seat venue. I wanted it to go so well. I called upon all my apprenticeship experience, from the dance floors on the Southern Shore to commanding the attention of noisy pubgoers in downtown St. John's.

I strode confidently to the mic to open the show, and two things struck me like a stone. There was no dance floor, and the audience was sitting quietly, looking right at us.

Shit.

The two main skill sets I'd developed over the past decade were little use to me in the cold, hard spotlight. More studying to do.

Greg Malone was the de facto ringmaster of the most influential band of my young life, The Wonderful Grand Band. Every time he interacted with the band, he did so with a mix of compliment and ribbing. Older Irish acts had more theatrical paths to front the band. Liam Clancy often strode onstage confidently and did a two-minute monologue that led to the first song. It was completely spellbinding.

And then there were the singers who led the night by completely occupying each song they delivered. Bruce Springsteen and Irish Folk God Christy Moore led the way with this. They often spoke or lightly bantered between songs, but when the song kicked in, they transported the audience from one world to the next as the circumstances of the song required.

Concerts held in a soft-seat theatre require a completely different cocktail. The patrons are seated, but they don't always want to be. Yet they did not pay for that plushy seat to have their view of the stage obscured by drunken punters in front of them. So I started arranging the set lists to allow for the rises and dips I thought would accommodate what most people would enjoy.

A pal once said, "Man, a GBS concert has more standing and sitting than Holy Sunday mass."

I started making lists of how the sets of songs were arranged in my favourite concerts—when did the front guy speak in between songs, and when did he link a bunch of songs together. I recalled that one of my favourite moments watching bands who were visiting St. John's at the Memorial Stadium was when they'd say, "Hey, great to be in St. John's. We walked the Signal Hill trail yesterday."

I made it a point to mention each night onstage at least one local experience I had in every town. It has served me so well since it forces me, in the rare occurrence that I am not in the mood, to get out and see the town each day. It has been great for my physical and mental health.

I love the rush of the first few songs—when you see the audience checking out what the stage looks like and they're happy to see the members of the band haven't changed or are curious about seeing a new member. I love the breath that comes after the first block of songs when I can chat with the room before the first ballad. I love setting a big, near show-stopping song right in the middle of the show, one that could easily mark the end of most concerts but not this one. I love the big fall into the second ballad at the two-thirds mark and the big buildup to the massive finale. I love coming back for the encore with one more trick up my sleeve like a special guest or having one of the other band members sing a song. And I love the one final simple song that just says thank you.

———

Over the years in clubs and pubs, in my uncle's band, during solo gigs in pubs or performing on the biggest stages in Canada with GBS or solo, I have committed almost every egregious error a front man can make. To list a few, I have:

- stood on a stage in Dublin, Ireland, and proclaimed, "Great to be in the UK!"
- insisted everyone in the house get on their feet, including the last hold-out fella, who to my great shame I would discover was in a wheelchair
- left the stage in Kingston, Ontario, to barf in a bucket because I was so sick from stomach flu.
- shouted, "Anybody here hungover from last night?" at a festival, only to realize we were playing the children's set
- forgotten the words in part or in whole to every song I've ever written or learned
- exclaimed in German that I was a Newfoundland Dog

• stood before audiences with every kind of wardrobe malfunction—every flying low and every bat in the cave. I have suffered them all.

You might think that these errors would be far in my past, and I wish you were correct. But in the winter of 2016 we had a three-song set at the Ann Arbor Folk Fest winter fundraiser. This was a multi-act, very folky affair in a posh theatre with small duos and trios coming and going around a mic or two. I figured we could make a bigger splash if we brought out the whole band with bass and drums and our big sound desk and all. We'd be the only super-pro-sounding, full-headline act to appear onstage. We'd win the night for sure.

Nope.

We strode onstage about four minutes too late, as our setup was longer than everyone else's. Without a proper sound check it took a song and a half to get our massive audio setup sounding right. All my banter was distracted by technical issues, and my content was more geared towards a beer garden than a quiet folk festival. By the time the third song came along—another boisterous rocker for a crowd hungry for mandolin and stories—we had lost them.

Bono got it right in Boston. Freddie got it right at Live Aid. I blew it in Ann Arbor.

But luckily, I have way more memories of elation than dejection from the spotlight. In my current, or recently current, touring outfit, I am surrounded by a dream team of musicians and companions. They lift me up and make me want to be better, and I see them do that for each other night after night. That's part of the rush and satisfaction of it all too. The feeling that the band and the audience are glad you've called them all together. To give each other their time and talents. It's not the first time and won't be the last time I say it, or shout to the heavens: "A crowd needs a band almost as bad as a band needs a crowd."

And we needed the crowd to stick with us some years back during a Great Big Sea concert in a Fredericton hockey rink when the entire electrical grid lost power. It was a real downer, since the band and four thousand fans were having the night of our lives. As the PA and lighting rig went down and the emergency lamps cast a cold, spell-breaking light across the room, our tour manager told me they'd need a five- to ten-minute break to switch to a generator.

I recalled the bravado of Freddie Mercury, the gratitude of Bono and Uncle Ronnie's rule to keep the dance floor full. I'd need the whole audience to keep this train on the rails.

"We don't need no break!" I shouted, and ran down-stage centre. I held my hands in the air and then against my lips, motioning everyone to hush for a second. To my surprise, they did. I knew I had one chance to hold the room, so I did not say a word. I just sang,

"Oh me, oh my, I heard me old wife cry." The opening chorus lyrics to the Newfoundland traditional song "Excursion Around the Bay" had been a singalong favourite at our concerts for a decade, and I figured it was my best chance to engage everyone and keep us all together now. I rolled the dice and prayed the hockey rink full of people would answer. And answer they did.

Four thousand people shouted, "Oh me, oh my," and off we went. What followed was a four- to five-minute incredible show of togetherness and commitment to a good night out from band and audience alike. In the cold emergency light, we sang the full song without amplification of any kind at all. Without fancy moving lights or any of the normal concert accoutrements, we sang and with each verse and chorus the energy grew almost as fast as the realization that we were all doing something very cool together that we could never do alone or over a phone call or a video conference meeting.

I added an extra chorus at the end, and with the luck that any good night needs, the power clicked back on as we hit the final notes. You could not have planned it better. The audience applauded me for my efforts, and I applauded them for theirs.

A mix of humility and confidence. You don't always get the blend right, but when you do, it is the best drink in the world.

———

I remain a student of the craft. Constantly looking and learning and gathering notions on how to reinvent the wheel. How to do the same thing differently. How to frame and present a set of songs in an order that makes the night something more than a recital. The best concerts have an ebb and flow. They rise and fall.

Here in these COVID-19 times, it pains me to talk and type about concerts, as I fear they are a ways away. Will governments ever allow such gatherings again? Will the audiences come back if they do? I am fearful but hopeful.

I daydream about standing at the side of the stage when the house lights are called. I'll be craning my neck around the corner and looking at the audience for any kind of insight I might glean about the best cocktail to serve.

Till the curtain calls, see you downstage centre.

LAST
CALL

I USED TO hate last call. And I often say I still do, as it fits the rock 'n' roll cliché and persona. But to be perfectly honest, I hear it now as a tolling that says "you did it." You did all there was to do. You saw it through to the end.

I do lament early closing hours on the road when musicians and restaurant staff roam the streets after their shifts, hoping to find one place still open, but at home the ringing of the bell is music to my ears. Like a prize fighter whose purse is earned not by winning or losing, but by going the distance.

So, thank you, Dear Reader, for going the distance with me on this, our imagined night in the pub. I am lucky in so many ways, but especially to have this outlet to chat and feel connected when connection is so hard to feel right now. I am as grateful as ever that you would give me your night, or afternoon, or morning. As I become keenly more and more aware that each of these times is a precious one, I thank you for sharing them with me to daydream or night dream about when we can all gather as we once did.

Till then, I hope these pages have made us feel what we need to feel.

All Together. Now.

Cheers,
Alan

I WOULD LIKE to thank all hands at Penguin Random House Canada for encouraging me to write this book. It was well into the spring of 2020 when they suggested I write a book of random stories to help both me and the readers through this most unprecedented time. They would need it written by mid-summer for a fall release. I was not sure I could do it. They were all most certain that I could, and I thank them for that confidence.

In particular, thanks to Scott Sellers and Martha Kanya-Forstner for getting the ball rolling and Tim Rostron and Ward Hawkes for keeping me on track. Also thanks to Kelly Hill for the wicked design.

As ever, many thanks to everyone at Sonic Entertainment,

especially Louis and Mel for suffering me and all the madness I bring into their lives so regularly.

All the thanks in the world to my Mom and Dad, and all the extended Doyle gang.

As ever and ever, thanks to Joanne and Henry for making every day a day worth having a thousand times over.

And most of all, thanks to you dear readers and anyone who has ever picked up one of my books or pressed play on any of my songs or given me a night of your time and lent me your voice at a gig somewhere out there.

I miss you terribly. I do.